THE REACH OF SONG, 1989–1990

Volumes of Poetry
published by

Georgia State Poetry Society, Inc.:

**A Book of the Charter Year,
August 30, 1979–1980**

The Reach of Song, Book 1

The Reach of Song, Book 2

The Reach of Song, Book 3

The Reach of Song, Book 4

The Reach of Song, Book 5

The Reach of Song, Book 6

The Reach of Song, Book 7

The Reach of Song, Book 8

**The Reach of Song
A Book of the Tenth Year
August 30, 1988–1989**

The Reach of Song, 1989–1990

**SHADOWDRIFTERS
Images of China**
A Prize-Winning Chapbook
By Patricia E. Canterbury

SUMMER AT THE DREAMLAND MOTEL
A Prize-Winning Chapbook
By Lethe Hunter Bishop

THE REACH OF SONG, 1989–1990

Jo Ann Yeager Adkins,
Editor

Charles B. Dickson,
Virginia P. Dickson,
Consulting Editors

Georgia State Poetry Society, Inc.

ACKNOWLEDGMENTS

The Reach of Song, 1989–1990 is supported in part by the Georgia Council for the Arts through the appropriations from the Georgia Assembly and the National Endowment for the Arts.

For permission to include copyrighted material, the following acknowledgments are gratefully made by Georgia State Poetry Society, Inc.

Richard G. Beyer: OPENING DAY, the Panhandler, Fall, 1990; Wil Carter: SPIDER WEAVER, Poems To Remember: Southern Poetry Review, Volume II, 1988; William L. Davenport: PUTTING ASUNDER, Georgia Journal, Spring 1990; Beverly Denmark: GROWING OLD, Parnassus Literary Journal, Winter 1989; Herbert Walter Denmark: STREET PEOPLE, Parnassus Literary Journal, Winter 1989; Charles B. Dickson: ELEGY FOR A MOUNTAIN POET, The Lyric, Volume 69, No. 4, 1989; Betty Lou Gore: CASTING, Parnassus Literary Journal, Spring, 1988; Connie J. Green: SONG FOR SPRING, Now and Then, The Appalachian Magazine, Volume 7, No. 1, Spring 1990; Elizabeth Ann Hammill: TREASURER, Seasons of the Wind, 1990, Society of American Poets; Jane L. Hart: THE SPIRITUAL DESERT, Seasons of the Wind, 1990, Society of American Poets; John T. Hendricks: CAROUSEL MAN, Cumberland Crossroads, 1988; Albert R. Horrell: TRAIL BLAZE, America's Best Amateur Poets of 1985, Johnson Publishing Co., 1985; Peggy Zuleika Lynch: RITUAL, Lucidity, A Quarterly Journal of Verse, Bear House Publishing, June 1990; June Owens: PIECES OF MOUNTAINS, Sandcutters, Arizona State Poetry Society, 1989; Denver Stull: THE HEIRLOOM, Grit, 1981; Memye Curtis Tucker: BONSAI, Lullwater Review, Volume I, No. 1, 1990; Memye Curtis Tucker: FROM HIS LIFE, The Southern Review, Volume 27, No. 3, 1991; Virginia Cole Veal: TABLEAU, Poetry Premiere, Southern Poetry Association; Golda Foster Walker: UNASSUMING KNIGHT, Riding With the Wind, A Collection of Sonnets, Lieb-Schott Publications 1985; Dorothy Williamson Worth: AMANDA IN STATE, Georgia State University Review, Winter 1990.

ISSN   0740-7521
ISBN   0-918279-16-X

Inquiries, accompanied by a self-addressed, stamped envelope, may be directed to:

Jo Ann Yeager Adkins, Editor
2826 Evansdale Circle N. E.
Atlanta, Georgia 30340

From chips and shards, in idle times,
I made these stories, shaped these rhymes;
May they engage some friendly tongue
When I am past the reach of song.

Byron Herbert Reece

CONTENTS

PRIZE POEMS

THE BYRON HERBERT REECE INTERNATIONAL POETRY AWARD

SPONSOR: Georgia State Poetry Society

JUDGE: Judson Jerome

FIRST: Memye Curtis Tucker
From His Life

SECOND: Dorothy Williamson Worth
Night Before The Auction

THIRD: Dorothy Williamson Worth
Villanelle for Autumn

FOURTH: Jeffrey DeLotto
A Voice From the Chapel

FIFTH: Pat Anthony
The Hill Women

SIXTH: Patsy Anne Bickerstaff
Bluejacket's Passage

HONORABLE MENTION:

Sandra Russell
The Godmother

Judith A. DeVries
The Long Jump

FROM HIS LIFE

Memye Curtis Tucker

Deafness is not silence. The high E piercing
the close of Smetana's E minor string quartet
was the note that rang in his head every moment
of his last years—no space in the composer's
mind not already jammed with sound. Think of

Monet straining against his own fingers
while the traitorous flowers blurred, think of dazed,
soaring Nijinsky, for whom pain's knife
was as daily as bread. What the body takes
is given back in vision, we want to believe—

desire old as our first knowledge of pain
longs to hear the enemy's voice subdued,
beaten into something of use—a fugue,
a twisting leap, pigment the color of flame.

NIGHT BEFORE THE AUCTION

Dorothy Williamson Worth

He walked through moon-drenched fields, the rows of corn
Like some gaunt scarecrow come to sudden life;
He paused outside the house where he was born,
The place he brought Miranda as his wife.
Each curve of stream, each polished rock, he knew;
The secret, moss-grown place where deer gave birth.
He'd watched each pine and dogwood as it grew
In season; he was one with this good earth.
At last he climbed the tallest hill and stood,
A fragile figure etched against the sky.
He drank the beauty of both field and wood,
Remembering the toil, the years gone by.
At dawn's first glow, the truth was plain to see:
This land would bloom again, and so would he.

VILLANELLE FOR AUTUMN

Dorothy Williamson Worth

Above the restless stream, the hills have turned to gold,
And morning sun seeks out a scarlet maple leaf;
But from the east a rising wind is blowing cold.

This valley, lately harvested, is brown and old.
The summer's verdant blossoming was all too brief;
Above the restless stream, the hills have turned to gold.

As I drink in the ripened world my eyes behold,
The thought that all lies dying is beyond belief;
But from the east a rising wind is blowing cold.

The taste of grape, the smell of muscadine, still hold,
Although the fields have given up their last pale sheaf.
Above the restless stream, the hills have turned to gold.

Wild aster fades as in a tragedy foretold;
This sky, this warming sun, might promise some relief—
But from the east a rising wind is blowing cold.

A winter's sleep, and then new petals will unfold:
But never these my fingers touch in solemn grief.
Above the restless stream, the hills have turned to gold,
But from the east a rising wind is blowing cold.

A VOICE FROM THE CHAPEL:
MISSION SAN ANTONIO DE VALERO; MARCH 6, 1836
COLONEL JAMES BOWIE TO HIS SLAVE

Jeffrey DeLotto

Where we die there's always rock and sky;
These walls, this earth and dirt—the old fox
Has run to ground, tooth and all.
Sam, hand old Mas'Jim that jug there—
You recall where this blade here
First found home in some man's ribs?
God, times I thought this steel pushing
Me west, quivering like a divining rod
But I see the tiny shells frozen here
In these dry stone blocks, and the pens,
The slave pens out on Galvez haunt me still;
The eyes of black faces rolling like worlds,
The waves washing nothing clean, not
Jean Lafitte smirking like an old baboon,
Fingering a stolen saber, selling souls
By the pound—and me buying a round
Bundle, too, under that sweaty sky.
Go, Sam—I set you free. Leave me
To dance to that damned deguello
Blown for us all, for the mission, the cause,
The call of men hungry for the ground,
Hungry to be sold into oblivion . . . .

No, leave the cob—me and the whiskey
Will race like old horses gone lame;
Why did I hostage my name to those
Arkansas acres, to Ursula's promise of peace,
To the fame of a cloud-gray blade
Made from a piece of falling sky?
Dammit, Sam—why do I lie here
On these greasy Kiowa rags, on this bag
Of corn husks for a cot, waiting to be shot
Or stuck by some indio zapadore?
I could have opened one belly more
And not be rustling here, coughing
And groaning like a lung-shot buck,
Here to end, with two trembling children
And a sack of breathing property

That may be but has not been;
God, Sam—the chains, the men,
The days spent like coins . . . .

THE HILL WOMAN

Pat Anthony

The hill woman

is rock chipped from Ozark hills that fall
away beneath her clotheslines and become
the river's thin blue ribbon slipping
swiftly over graveled bars between
the snags. Caught in the mallard's startled
mouth. Filtered with Osage bottom silt

replicating the way she riffles
through years passed in this dark valley of
something other than contentment. Hands
sharp as talons bear testimony.
Claw holds in unforgiving faces.
Piece autumns to icy winters. Grip

the ancient pickup's bucking wheel, its
turnings unpredictable as those
children fallen from her womb into
this dark crevasse. The youngest pinned by
tractor's weight below the ridge. Her hands
powerless to lift or still the spinning

air rent by his once and anguished scream.
To find faith for her oldest daughter
who left upon the convent steps black
habits, married, moved to another state.
Her middle son thick as a burr oak;
sullen, never taking women, so
that she finds her fingers aching for

the small helplessness of swaddled forms
even as she gathers laundry from
the line; frozen, harsh against her skin.
Inside, dampness rises, a slow cold
given off by the folded pile bent
across the chair's back. Her breath quickens,

twisted fingers redden in the space
heater's glow. Silently, her husband

16

pads from the kitchen, coffee beading
In his red beard. She sets the iron
to warm now. Watches as he filches
one sock, then the next from the fender.

Feels him squeeze her skinny bottom as
he passes. Knows his mind, already gone
beyond any thought of her on to
cows waiting in the lower pasture,
their lowing that leaves her hands empty;
his full of pink udders, waiting teats.

BLUEJACKET'S PASSAGE

Patsy Anne Bickerstaff

He crouches at the seawall, staring long
With drenched, transparent eyes, beyond foamcrests
Of tidewhipped waves, beyond blood-tinted streaks
Of sunset, at steel memories of ships
On pencilled gray horizon, real as fog.
His wraith sails with them, on the sea again,
Discarding boyhood all too eagerly,
The ruby in his ear, his slanted smile
Disguises of bravado for his youth.
He lives cramped, restless nights, the fights, dice, lies
That punctuated monotones of dark;
Days chapped by hot salt wind, that cured his skin
And hypnotized with wandercries of gulls
That haunt a lifetime; gasps with echoed fear
Of metal rain from clouds of fire, of death
In myriad costumes, stalking ships like game,
Retches at mutilated flesh, at screams
From parts of faces; walks an alleyway
Through stench of spice and rot; past corpses, whores
And naked urchins; clatter, bleating, shrieks
Like creaking hinges; tastes of bitter smoke.
He finds her narrow door, her crescent eyes,
Those incense hours, like watercolored birds;
Kneels at her side once more, to bring the world
The miracle they made; that nowhere child
Has children, too, by now, or else is dead.
His hand is brown and crumpled as the bag
He clutches, on the bottle. It is here,
This other, amber ocean, where he drowns
His yesterdays, a thousand times; those pains
The world will not permit a man to feel.
He cannot quench the siren-whine of gulls
Pulling like tides; he cannot dim the moon
Whose ghostlight dances, teasing, beckoning,
Skipping the frail meniscus of the sea.

DR. JOHN RANSOM LEWIS, JR. AWARD
Poet Laureate of Georgia

SPONSOR: Mikki Griffis Morris

JUDGE: Jack Murphy

FIRST: Charles B. Dickson
          Radiance of a Unicorn

SECOND: Ellen Dugan
          Nursing Home

THIRD: Jeanne Losey
          Attic Memories

RADIANCE OF A UNICORN

Charles B. Dickson

Doe-nimble and swift, you plunged
that bright June morning,
under hemlocks and birches,
down the slope below Flycatcher Falls.
Your laughter burnished the breeze
like birdsong. And when I overtook you,
you were kneeling by the tremulous waters
of a spring, cupped palm at your lips,
dripping fragments of light.
I, too, knelt and drank. We sprawled
in the shade of lilac-purple blossoms
of Catawba rhododendron.
                              "A place
of enchantment! Perfect for newlyweds!"
you said. I answered capriciously,
ad libbing as I spoke, "How right you are!
Local legend says this spring is magic,
transforming all who drink of it, sooner
or later, into fabulous creatures.
No one escapes."
                    At those words, you sprang
to your feet, prancing and tossing
your fair hair like a mane. "It has happened
already!" you cried. "I am a unicorn
and you are a centaur!"
                         And I remember,
though fifty years have slowed you
to a stately step, that you were
a capering unicorn and I a centaur
the rest of that radiant day.

NURSING HOME

Ellen Dugan

The frail stranger in Room 709
was my aging father's best friend
for two and a half hours
one Sunday afternoon
last April
when they sat outside together
and talked about spring flowers,
the rising price of gasoline and
I can't remember what else
exactly
Except that the words were important enough
to save my father's life
for three more days
as he rocked away
his loneliness
and remembered who I was
between the pauses
of our last good-bye
before the rain

ATTIC MEMORIES

Jeanne Losey

A musty attic, dark and drear,
With memories stored away,
Mementos of somebody's hopes
And dreams of yesterday.
A trunk that holds a packet of
Love letters tied in blue,
Some photographs, a wedding dress,
A tiny baby shoe.
A dainty linen handkerchief
That's edged in lace so fine
Is folded in a card that says,
"Please be my Valentine."
A wedding ring, a lock of hair,
The dog tags that he wore,
A box that holds a purple heart
Earned on a foreign shore.
A ribbon with three little words,
Just "Rest In Peace" in gold,
A flag that graced a casket lid,
The mournful story told.
Old memories that are stored away
May fade but never die.
So many attics hide the dreams
And pain of days gone by.

LAURRAINE GOREAU MEMORIAL POETRY AWARD

SPONSOR: Mary Anne DeVillier
Mary Martha Glazebrook

JUDGE: John Dean Vaughn

FIRST: Thelma R. Hall
Going Home

SECOND: Thelma R. Hall
Epiphany

THIRD: June Owens
Aria for my Singer
(Pavarotti: Live at the Charlotte Colosseum)

HONORABLE MENTION:

Mavis H. Harrell
Beach Scene

June Owens
Fantasia for Tunesmith and Alto Sax

Charles Dickson
The Silent Clock

Glenda B. LaGarde
Metaphysics at Kale's Swamp

Thelma R. Hall
The Wolf is at my Door

GOING HOME

Thelma R. Hall

Four lanes split billboards and trees;
tall nodding grasses beard balding slopes.
Two lanes curve past houses with porches,
Rock City barns and Get Right With God yards.
One lane roads send dust clouds flying
over sagging houses; near-sighted hens
squint in the yards.
Sweat runs down into
landscapes of flesh-
Deep rutted paths
tangled in vines
narrow memory—
No one is home here,
but behind,
the road is obscured
and I cannot return.

EPIPHANY

Thelma R. Hall

It was an ordinary night
except that he had forgotten the garbage.
Slippered, robed, he began the task.
Cans rattled and neighboring dogs
barked their disapproval.
Cats followed the scent of tuna,
the unearthly blending of juices and pulp.
A gush of water hosed down
the offending can.
And then the extraordinary sky
caught him off guard.
There, as clear as if beamed
upon a screen, Glorified Andromeda
gleamed above him, loosed from her chains.
He traced her lines
with his naked eyes,
felt the immensity of sky upon sky,
while the small earth's refuse
accumulated unnoticed
around his feet.

ARIA FOR MY SINGER
(Pavarotti: Live at the Charlotte Colosseum)

June Owens

You sang to me while I
Planted gardens, but you did not know.
The tapes turned round and round,
Sheltered me from the world's cold wisdom,
The honest sun's insanity.
For each seed set down, I said:
For you. For me.
And when the pinewoods wind
Went down my sprouting rows,
I thought we had made good music.
We came together in such ways
As poems cannot tell.
I sang along with you:
   Non ti scordar di me . . .
Your voice soared, mine wobbled.
But the day did not mind
And the sun made allowances.

Now I sit in this concert hall,
Far and high in an airless balcony.
A forest of people sits between us.
Feet scuffle and programs pulsate.
I listen to you through little
Binoculars that tremble and blur you
With my heart's poundings.
I lip the words you sing,
Send them back to you.
But it is not the same:
   Too many breaths breathe.
   Too many hands applaud.
   I do not have your music to myself.
   Why do the songs stop?
   Will they rise again like bridges
   For our comprehension?
   Perhaps we need the sanctity
   Of sun and soil,
   Pine winds and gardens,
   We who only listen.

I KNEW I COULD DO IT AWARD

SPONSOR: Charles and Virginia Dickson

JUDGE: Sheila Whitfield

FIVE FIRST PRIZES AWARDED:

Pat Dozier
C.D.

Betty Lou Gore
No Miracle Today

Leonard Paul Harris
Remembrance of a Dear Place

Paula L. Stricklin
I Never Got to Dance For You

Ethelene Dyer Jones
**Sonnet on a Poet's Early Death
(In Memory of Byron Herbert Reece,
1917–1958)**

C.D.

Pat Dozier

Hey there, China Doll!
Can you hear us as we call?
Look around and you will see
The world was watching on T.V.
Your beauty and your youthful grace,
Your hopes and dreams shown on your face.
You have to know that we were there.
We have had our Tiananmen Square;
We saw your Lady, proud and tall,
Reaching for freedom for you all.
Smashed and gone, but in her place
A sacred spot for you to face
The future, as you know you will
Although it be a poison pill.
Doll of China, dry your tears,
Teach them how to face their fears.
Tell them how they have to try
Although your comrade had to die.
Our hearts are breaking at your plight.
We pray that things will turn out right.
Scale Heaven's Gate—on to the wall.
We'll greet you there—brave China Doll!

NO MIRACLE TODAY

Betty Lou Gore

When they handed me your ashes
In a small, book-shaped container,
Numbly I looked at it, knowing
Full well there was nothing to read,
The last chapter had been written,
The book of your life was closed . . .
And I sat there remembering
The first time you were handed to me,
A small, red, blue-eyed miracle,
Screaming for comfort at my breast . . .
Where had the years gone, I wondered,
Why was there no miracle today?

"REMEMBRANCE OF A DEAR PLACE"

Leonard Paul Harris

My father, the child, recalls for me
A summer of exquisite loneliness
And almost unbearable melancholy:

It was the first time that wise youth
Had encountered either phenomenon
Except as the wistful searching
Of an eternally disaffected child,
Terrified even then by the bewildering
Change in time, change in place
That would haunt the restless man
He would become at too early an age.

That summer of arbors and bowers,
Towers of pines and vined jungles—
The only such summer my father,
The child, ever was to know—
Was the gateway between youth,
His innocence, and adulthood
With its withering wisdoms and wits.

He isolated himself in the emerald
Of summer, a cocoon of being
He was to return to in fact
And in fancy for four decades,
To emerge in the decadence of fall
An adult overcoated in jade.

His once was summer's opulence
Under Georgia's fraudulent blue skies,
His only escape into nature's innocence
And a time, a place of incomparable fiction.

I NEVER GOT TO DANCE FOR YOU

Paula L. Stricklin

The night you left
You called my name
Somewhere beyond a veil of trains.
I did not rouse
But lay instead beneath
A throw of memories weaved with
Promises of your return—
You always said in urgent tone
That you would have to leave—
I felt a numbness
Take your place beside me.
It stayed my escort
Through a desert of daylight hours
Till after midnight
When I watched for you
In the corners of my room,
Searching among the trails of moonlight
And clothes strewn on the chair—
You always said in urgent tone
You would return—
Somehow I dozed
Along the surface of faceless dreams
When suddenly you shook me
With an urgency
That should have made me rouse.

In early pain of morn
I sit with wordless pen in hand
Staring from my desk
At the world still breathing,
The garden still birthing,
And there on my favorite tree
I see where you carved
Your nose and eyeglasses
And I cry.
I never got to dance for you
Or build a barn with you;
What's worse, I never said goodbye
And I'm still here waiting,
Riveted to earth.

SONNET ON A POET'S EARLY DEATH
(In Memory of Byron Herbert Reece, 1917–1958)

Ethelene Dyer Jones

Dreamer of the impossible dream,
Oh, poet, whose spring is dry;
May your lines their penetrable gleam
To my mind insuppressibly cry.
For long at the well you drank
And nurtured your Muse with the draught;
But, alas, your memory fell blank
As steel forced your words to a halt.
In ceaseless reminder they lie,
These lines penned in passion's duress;
For thoughts like the limitless sky
You captured with cunning repress.
Black on white lies in culminate rows
Your depths and your heights to expose.

PEN AND PICA LITERARY SOCIETY AWARD

SPONSOR: Pen and Pica Arts Clayton, Inc., Clayton
County, Georgia

JUDGE: Don Russ

FIRST: Alma C. Brown
Coming Back to the Golden Isles

SECOND: Dorothy Williamson Worth
Picasso Envisions *Guernica*

THIRD: Georgia Henry
Questioned Reliance

COMING BACK TO THE GOLDEN ISLES

Alma C. Brown

Year after year, after year,
We gather our encumbrances and come back here
Where the golden grasses bend
And flow with the warm wind.
The palms and stunted pines
Steadfastly creep to hold their stand
Where the waves fall over against the glinting sand.

Our footsteps clatter down the wooden walk.
The old ones lead their dogs, while overhead,
The clamoring gulls circle and swoop to snatch
From the wary children's hands their scraps of bread.
A boat comes in, a boat goes slowly out and dissolves
Where sea and sky become one.
And for a moment, our pensive faces are bathed
In the last scarlet rays of the sun.
With blurring eyes in the cooling mist,
We watch the lumbering pelicans go by,
Skimming the blue-gray water
Under the gray-blue sky.
Even the youngest children know
What lies beyond "the boundless, deep blue sea";
Yet as we seek the evening lights of the town,
We are haunted by some ancient, unsolved mystery.

One morning early, we gather our worthless
    shells and books unread,
Over the causeway, over the burnished marsh,
Our thoughts are our own. No words are said.
Then into the swaying Georgia pines, we meet the
    silver rain,
And we know that if our small world holds,
Next year, we will come to the Golden Isles again.

PICASSO ENVISIONS *GUERNICA*

Dorothy Williamson Worth

Paint war
without standards   no
flags unfurled   without
warriors   no
poppy fields
and no
Elysium.

Paint spring
without green   no
sun   laughter
cut off under
black walls   light
insufficient   density
chaos.

Paint fear
in forms
shattered   a child
torn   a
horse screaming
women
fallen.

Paint death
black-and-
white   no
crimson   not
flesh   but
shapes in
monochrome.

Paint hell
with white
flames   not the
ten thousand
but nine   a box
window   a
door closed.

QUESTIONED RELIANCE

Georgia T. Henry

I never needed a daughter—
never wished for one—until now.
As I sit waiting in doctors' offices
watching daughters escort aging mothers
to appointments, I am saddened
at my lack, wondering
who will take care of me
in my infirmity.
I think of my mother at these times.
Know the oneness of child and mother.
Yet, when I turn it around
to mother and son, me and mine—
I'm left with me
and possibly another:
"A son is a son until he takes a wife,
but a daughter is a daughter all of her life."

Is it the remembrance of my absent father,
when the doctor asked for my nearest of kin—
and he sent my stepmother, his second wife,
to minister to my questioned life?
Is my longing misplaced? The child
in me wanting mothering? Is it my mother
I miss? The ministering to her. The yearning
for security I feel that results
in waiting room companionship I find unreal.

My sons were by my bedside
when I last called out in fear;
why should I have this anxiety
when they would again appear?

GWENDOLYN BROOKS AWARDS

SPONSOR: Herbert W. Denmark

JUDGE: Melanie Rawls Abrams

FIRST: Mary Catherine Comiskey
Vacation South

SECOND: June E. Foye
Cold Day on Fourth Avenue

THIRD: Leisa Coulter
Memories of Times Past

VACATION SOUTH

Mary Catherine Comiskey

Her tiny brown frame
is but a display rack for
straw hats and plastic toys.
She hustles away her youth
for ten pesos, or twenty,
or thirty please sir.

Her market place opens
when the wealthy come South
all floral and smiling.
The man with his camera,
the wife with her tan,
amused by the simple souvenirs
all for ten pesos, or twenty,
or thirty please sir.

One sale, I eat not.
Two sales, some dry beans.
Three sales, a bone bare blanket
to shelter my seldom sleep.

For ten pesos, or twenty,
or thirty please sir, please.
Purchase my childhood,
Help buy my dirty day.

COLD DAY ON FOURTH AVENUE

June E. Foye

He loiters
as if he's stood forever on street corners
and, seduced by dullness,
has forgotten to resent
the days' identical profiles.
His young face carries old denials
that a Phoenix could arise—
or any happy legend—out of ashes.

His jacket seems a plaything for the wind.
I wonder how many coats he's worn
that cried their thinness;
how many twisters have laid waste
the land of the inside boy;
and is there any shelter
he can huddle in?

MEMORIES OF TIMES PAST

Leisa Coulter

I lie in an iron bed
        wrinkles multiply, pulse lessens.

Birth of a child
        bright blue eyes.

White lace of a white gown
        beautiful flowers surround me.

I see him for the first time.
        Love.

The diploma in my hand,
        my name echos through the crowd's applause.

A skinned-up knee on a brand new bike
        Mom's kisses soothe the pain.

Learning to walk.
Learning to crawl.

        Helpless.

MAREL BROWN AWARD

SPONSOR: Betty Lou Gore

JUDGE: Leslie Mellichamp

FIRST: June Owens
The Horse of Time

SECOND: Charles B. Dickson
Ascent from Hades

THIRD: Charles B. Dickson
The Final Sip

THE HORSE OF TIME

June Owens

Because I do not hope to turn again
  To sounds of love I know will not be there,
I neither will acknowledge nor explain
  These wisps of breath that blow upon my hair.

To sounds of love I know will not be there,
  The spinning silence, some remembered touch,
These wisps of breath that blow upon my hair
  I give forgiveness, but, then, not too much.

The spinning silence. Some remembered touch.
  Oh, move away, that dreams may gather sleep.
I give forgiveness (but, then, not too much)
  For all the useless passions running deep.

Oh, move away, that dreams may gather sleep,
  You crippled horse of time, now riderless.
For all the useless passions running deep,
  There is no answer, reason, or caress.

You crippled horse of time, now riderless,
  What perishes is no concern of yours;
There is no answer, reason, or caress
  Can change the smell of loss, or settle scores.

Love's voice may come, love's visions congregate;
  I neither will acknowledge or explain.
Old loves must die. Old melodies must wait
  Because I do not hope to turn again.

NOTE: The line, "Because I do not hope to turn again," is from *Ash Wednesday*, by T. S. Eliot.

42

ASCENT FROM HADES

Charles B. Dickson

Head aching and his drunken wager won,
a sober Orpheus trudges toward the sun.
He dimly can recall the bet he made,
wits numbed by wine, disporting in a glade,
that he could pluck his lyre with such great skill
grim Pluto would relent, filled by goodwill.
He scarcely grasps that all is now attained,
the miracle performed, his wife regained.

The magic of his lyre had so entranced
dread Cerberus the guardian beast had danced
and fawned while Orpheus entered Hades' gate
with tipsy unconcern about his fate.
Inside, the singing strings so mesmerized
the god of death that he had authorized
his minions to release Eurydice.
The god had thundered he would set her free
if Orpheus pledged that he would not look back
upon the wife who followed in his track
till both emerged into the light of day,
no longer subject to fierce Pluto's sway.

So it has been. The bet is won. But now
more than a few misgivings crease his brow.
Before her death, he recollects, his wife
had been the source of much familial strife,
jealous of nymphs, inclined to sulk and nag
each time he stumbled homeward on a jag.

His tongue is parched. He thinks of bowls of wine
and playful naiads under oak and pine.
How vividly he now recalls her glare!
He wheels about and pins her with a stare.

THE FINAL SIP

Charles B. Dickson

Corrosion gnaws his ax and scythe and plough,
    His spade and hoe.
His fields lie choked by weed and sapling bough.
    His slow feet go
Unsurely up the trail. He stops to lean
    Against a fir,
Inhales the fragrance of wild wintergreen.
    Cicadas whir
On every side. White-throated sparrows sound
    Their plaintive songs
From laurel boughs. White featherbells abound
    And rosebay throngs
The rocky slopes with purple-lilac bloom.
    He is content,
Though drained by time and drawing near the tomb.
    A hawk's ascent
Attracts his gaze. He smiles to watch it wing.
    These are the links
That bind his world, these blooms and birds of spring.
    The old man thinks:
I drink my bedtime toddy, never waste
    The smallest nip,
And I will savor life until I taste
    The final sip.

EMILY DICKINSON AWARD

SPONSOR: Mary Ann Coleman

JUDGE: LaVerne Rison

FIRST: Wil Carter
Anastasia

SECOND: June Owens
The Unknown Face

THIRD: Dorothy Williamson Worth
Dimensions

ANASTASIA

Wil Carter

Poor mad Anastasia
dancing a waltz
    in a ballroom of your mind

The bloody gunshots are now muffled
    as faraway thunder
        and you can't see the clouds
        for the film in your eyes

Your teeth are bad
and your feet lame
    but waltz away, waltz away
        inside your brain
The giddy vision holds you close
    and you feel his press
and the gunshots are squirrels
        chittering in trees
    and the screams are the laughter
        of children at Christmas
The Nutcracker King still visits
        and calls you by name
and you waltz away
        waltz away
          waltz away
inside your brain

Lenin wanted the world
Lenin said such bitter things
    packed the family off
        to an unknown camp
But Anastasia!   gliding with poise and grace
        down the stair
    to the ball
    Smile and bow
        and kiss the Pope!
The bells of St. Mary's
    they give you such hope
        to waltz away   waltz away
        the end of your rope

And Anastasia, if you still want to dance
when the nurse stops the band,
why   waltz away
waltz away
waltz away
waltz away

THE UNKNOWN FACE
(For Emily Dickinson)

June Owens

Barefoot voice,
The braided beast remains,
Basks inside the barn
Of violated privacy,
Slides past picked over,
Packed up clothes.

Your letter, license,
Tolling drum, foxgloved summer, and
Your landlord grass nonetheless prevail.

Still your insects sip
Their little sips
Of brew, your ale words
Mulled because you chose to sing
Against your times
And all those Calvinists.

The buzz of night
Becomes a sodden sun
Whose silver rainfall
Sits on dazzled day,
Leaks life that slows to death,
And binds your poems
In bundles of dismay.

And now, nearby, its bee sting breath
Respires—at my own door
There waits that white
And staring, unknown face.

DIMENSIONS

Dorothy Williamson Worth

Shakespeare's prince
envisioned a nutshell
Dante imagined
an eternity of levels
Sartre saw fate
in the shape of a wall
Borges made a labyrinth
of a single straight line—

From out of the mists
that shroud the void
only the dreamer
catches a glimpse
of destiny's form.

SHORT AND SWEET CONTEST

SPONSOR: Walker's Shortbread of Scotland

JUDGE: Lamar York

GRAND PRIZE WINNER:

Nancy Treu Klotz
The Marrow of the Country

RUNNERS-UP:

FIRST: Mary Gage Davidson
Ferns

SECOND: Debra Hiers
Red Toes I

THIRD: Jeanne Osborne Shaw
The Sweetness of Life

FOURTH: John Ottley, Jr.
Looking for the Sweet

FIFTH: John Ottley, Jr.
Life is Sweeter

THE MARROW OF THE COUNTRY

Nancy Treu Klotz

Deep in my heart I'm city bred,
But like the marrow of the country
With my small town amigos
And their folk-like ways,
It is there unacquainted I became a friend.

The country has a florid complexion,
Untainted, with soft delicate hues
Lingering in my heart
Like picturesque undisturbed fields of yesteryear,
And I know I am not a stranger.

FERNS

Mary Gage Davidson

Pale, delicate, and green under dusty brown cape,
The velvet fern frond uncurls in escape.

Unfurling to reach what is lively and warm,
Fragile tendrils grow stronger, yet vulnerable to harm.

My hands like these ferns reach out softly to you.
And I shiver in fear—is it Spring here, too?

RED TOES I

Debra Hiers

Virgin toes painted red
for the first time at 30
remind me of the candy counter
at Burdine's when I was 8
and nothing but chocolate
mattered

THE SWEETNESS OF LIFE

Jeanne Osborne Shaw

The many hours in which we work are "salt,"
Yet they may bring the good that we exalt.
Our feeling for false friends may be quite "bitter,"
Yet it requires forgiveness that is fitter.
Reactions to our ills and hurts are "sour,"
Yet they bring patience, wisdom into flower.
Thus, since these tastes don't have to bring defeat,
The only one that really counts is "sweet!"

LOOKING FOR THE SWEET

John K. Ottley, Jr.

I listened for the sweetness of life
in a caged bird's song,
but heard it clearly when I let him free.
I sought sweetness between your thighs,
but found it in your tender handclasp.
I liked the taste of sweetness when
they put "vice president" on my door,
but still hungered for my lost dreams.
I thought the power of facts was sweet.
Ah, feelings, love, are sweeter still.

LIFE IS SWEETER

John K. Ottley, Jr.

When you don't:
  insist that your poems rhyme or
your friends fit into neat little boxes;
  set up housekeeping in the uppermost turret
of castle righteousness;
  confuse your beliefs with The Truth;
  fart on the first date;
  let love rust into resignation;
  or starve in the process
of feeding others.

ELLIS ATKINSON MACDONALD AWARD

SPONSOR: Helen Carnes

JUDGE: Anne George

FIRST: Charles B. Dickson
Love Poem

SECOND: Dorothy Williamson Worth
On the Glacier

THIRD: Charles B. Dickson
The Red-Tailed Hawk Still Soars

LOVE POEM

Charles B. Dickson

Early morning is the worst . . .
Dawn,
when he gropes awake
without defenses.
He listens for her breathing.
Silence.
He stretches out his hand,
an automatic gesture
after sixty years.
He encounters emptiness
between cool sheets.

He remembers . . .

He remembers
her turning toward him
sleepily,
pressing against him,
bending her knee
and placing the warmth
of her thigh
across his body.
He remembers
her head on his shoulder
in the crook of his arm,
her forehead against his cheek,
the rhythm of her breath
against his throat,
the murmured accounts
of her dreams.

He remembers too much.
Early morning is the worst.

ON THE GLACIER

Dorothy Williamson Worth

Nothing prepared me for this terrain.

No break appears, no projecting stone
no rough place to put my hand
Only the treachery of frozen glass
beneath my feet.
I cannot move up or down.

Behind,
just at the edge of this white field,
I can see the flowers
the green grass
and the mirrored lake.

Ahead
the grey escarpment looms
too steep to hold the winter's snow
exposed forever to the will
of wind and sun.

I am trapped
between the nubile slopes,
the summer melt,
and these granite peaks
that have escaped the clutch
of ice, and rise
in scarred and silent isolation
toward the sky.

THE RED-TAILED HAWK STILL SOARS

Charles B. Dickson

Now, one of us forgets the life we shared.
  Accumulated years have quenched the flame
That burned so brightly when you kissed and cared.
  You sit and do not even know your name.
The red-tailed hawk still soars in majesty
  And constellations wheel across the night.
The rose invites the hummingbird and bee,
  But all are lost to your Alzheimer's sight.
Such splendor once inspired your poet's pen
  To harmonies that rivaled harp and flute
And clothed in beauty mountain, marsh and wren.
  I stroke your cheek and grieve your muse is mute.
With snow or larkspur, this I strive to do:
Embrace enough magnificence for two.

MELISSA MARIE HENRY AWARD

SPONSOR: Georgia T. Henry

JUDGE: Donna Thomas

FIRST: Ellen Dugan
Help

SECOND: Pat Morton Posey
Katie

THIRD: Jeanne Osborne Shaw
Cafeteria Worker

HONORABLE MENTION:

FIRST: R. Riherd Greene
Spirit Impaired

SECOND: N. B. Bagato
The Haunt

THIRD: William Henry Williams
The Beautiful Bride

HELP

Ellen Dugan

Hold on, please
says a push-button voice
after I dial

(It is interrupted
begrudges me the please
then departs with a hurried click for its next assignment)

I can't
I scream silently
at the holding-on music

a can of sounds
left alone to fill in the quiet
while I wait

but there is no quiet for me
I am not able to hear it
Too much other noise is playing

inside my head
right now. Drums and a brass band beating
louder and louder with the trumpets

singing off key on purpose loud mocking songs
Please turn the volume down
I tell them all

How can I hear with the
"Stars and Stripes
Forever" marching through my head

at speeds I cannot follow
I plead with the holding-on music to put me through
knowing that it is dead

Don't you see I cry
The chorus is about to end
Soon there will be no more quiet verses left

(I try my best to explain it
but my thoughts keep laughing and jeering at me
telling me the sun is crying raindrops

and I must count each one before it hits the ground
and then there are blades of grass to count
and grains of sand and I must do it all by 3:00 o'clock

this afternoon or else I will stop thinking forever
and become quiet and dead as a gray stone
unless I do it all exactly right)

No mistakes
Oh please I cry I need a piece of paper
to begin. I have to hurry

Time is running out the trumpet voices say
Soon
yours will be all gone

But wait
Please wait for me
to finish

You must, they say
You have
no choice

I know
I must
I will

By 3 o'clock
See, I'm getting started
Right now this very minute

I hurry hurry
Where is the paper?
I cannot find it

Where is it
It must be here
I have to find it

I have to I must
be calm right now and
then I'll look for it again

But your time
the voices remind me ever so gently now
is almost up

and did you know, they whisper
Your sanity is leaving
in exactly ten minutes?

on a long trip
Do you want to go
to the beach on vacation

We hear the water's very nice this time of year
You need to pack
We have your ticket ready

Seat 16A
by the window
an excellent location

and it's never going to rain you silly stupid fool
Don't you know a joke that's cool
It's a rule you learned in school

and don't think your eyes won't blink
in a wink
when we wash you down the sink

They laugh uncontrollably
louder and louder
rolling over on their sides

screaming hysterically
until I have to hold my ears
to make them stop

My thoughts tumble over each other like modern dancers
forgetting what comes next. They
stop to look for the suntan lotion

tear the medicine cabinet apart to find it
see the elevator-music pills
in half-empty plastic that is smiling

on the bottom shelf
beckoning to me
with peaceful quiet

Its okay, they say
We're your only friends today
and we can help you go away

No I can't go
not today I say
I'm too afraid

I begin to sweat
My hands are wet
I think the telephone is going to electrocute me

But, if I go
I whisper
Pleading with the panic not to come out so loudly

Can I hear the sound of
Real words
Quiet ones

Connecting to each other
Making sense inside my head
Giving me directions

before I leave
Can you help me
please

You mean
Strangers who don't
Laugh

Scream
Cackle
Shout

Demand
More of you
Than we do? the hurt voices ask

Yes I cry
Please
Let me have a piece of quiet rope

to hold onto
before I let go
This time

for good and
then I promise
I'll come back again

(I know they wait like jackals
ready to eat the scraps but I have to
make this bargain. It is the only way)

But we are very hungry now
they laugh
We need to eat

Yes I know I say
But wait
Please

We can't wait they scream
Your time is running out
We have no rope

And what about the raindrops?
Grass?
and grains of sand? they ask

Turning mean
Menacing
Deadly

Did

You

Think

They pause
slowly
Each word cuts deep

a searing knife
they often
use

That we

Would

Forget?

Oh no,
Never
I didn't I knew but . . .

I beg them to please leave
Stop
Go away

Leave me alone
No more shouting
I cannot hear you

I will not listen anymore
I won't
I'll kill you first

My words only make them laugh
louder, faster, more raucous than before
like lunatics

running rampant
charging full speed ahead
leaving giant footprint holes across my skull

I try to quiet them
with threats—elevator music
like in the past

But they do not listen
this time. They
are not afraid

I try again
But they grow stronger louder
more powerful than before

One more try
is all there is left
But it is no use

They are too loud
It is too hard
I am too tired

Suddenly they stop
The holding-on music stops
It is quiet

A new voice
dressed in a long white coat
begins to talk

May I help you? it asks
(I think it really wants to)
Are you real? I answer

Straining to hear amid
the chaos that has begun again
fearing all the while that

it is not possible
There is no way out for me
except sleep

Yes, I'm real the new voice says
I hang up slowly
unable to hold on any longer

I have to feed the jackals
find my bathing suit
and take the elevator home

KATIE

Pat Morton Posey

Death can come to spirits
and their bodies be alive.
I am in a room with Death.
She has dark and moving eyes.

She has listening eyes, glassy but dead,
staring at every word that is said.
She has eyes on the wall, eyes of a fly,
watching footsteps tiptoe by,
counting stitches on rickrack,
fingers creeping to each thread,
eyes without passion, stunted, red
eyes without tears—no tears to shed
but swallowed poison of defeat,
lonely eyes, never to meet
one love-glance; eyes that follow,
never to see, stark and hollow,
suffering eyes- not blind-
eyes that lock some terror behind,
silent screaming death eyes.

Death can come to spirits
and their bodies be alive.
I am in a room with Death.
She has dark and empty eyes.

CAFETERIA WORKER

Jeanne Osborne Shaw

They say she's retarded; it's true
She has a silly, happy look on her face,
As if unaware the world needs pepper
And the coffee has long since grown cold.

She hurries around, unknowing she makes it hard
For the more able employees to measure up.
Someone at our table comments dourly,
"She can't even tell you if the cafeteria
Will be open on the Fourth of July."

But she asks if we need some pepper sauce;
Pushes the coffee cart around
To see who's half or even a quarter empty
And wants to make us whole.
"Enjoy it," she says, like a highly paid hostess,
Whereas the cashier up front
Looks as though she hopes we'll get ptomaine.

Perhaps this waitress knows something we don't
And has a feeling not subject to vagaries
Of seasoning in dishes and temperature of drinks.

SHORT NARRATIVE POEM CONTEST

SPONSOR: Marthalou Hunter

JUDGE: Carol Schott Marino

FIRST: Georgia T. Henry
            The Moving Wall: On View the Last Day

SECOND: Charles B. Dickson
            Eve

THIRD: Edward DeZurko
            Parental Guidance: Ronnie's Secret Bouquet

THE MOVING WALL: ON VIEW THE LAST DAY

Georgia T. Henry

I was not prepared for my reaction
on viewing the half-scale Washington, D.C. replica
listing the missing or killed.
We went to the memorial out of curiosity
just as we went to the same park
for the hoopla Classic Coke 100th Anniversary.
I went there with mixed emotions,
a remnant from the era
I was rearing my own son to hit, only if in return,
and to stay out of a fight unless he won.

My first glimpse of the rough raw boards
that backed The Wall gave me a foreboding feeling.
They seemed to be balanced in mid-air.
An unfinished pine structure
standing in the middle of Auchswitz.
As we crept closer behind this sidewards boardwalk,
peering around the other side,
we saw a green striped tent
and sensed a festive atmosphere
ballooning into air.

While juggling hot dogs and chips,
men, women and children were hawking leaflets.
Sponsored by MCI, WGST and Newstalk 92,
the carnival collided with reality
when I opened the handout
and skimmed a chronological directory of names.
Two teen-age boys were moving about
and making rubbings of names
on the leaflet space designated for such.

Scattered among the columns
were occasional messages of flowers,
fresh and dried, a single red rose,
miniature American flags
alongside scribbled notes
composed for everyone's eyes.
Poems portrayed undying affection
that stayed alive during the passage of time

72

when a nation was split
between condemning those who fought
and condemning those who fled.

I look at the veterans lolling around the area,
the special one in a wheelchair,
the paraplegic extolling independence
but void of legs.
Another one looking for his buddies in engraved words.
The frantic girl girded with pride
as she rushes in
to begin her search before it is too late.

The scene reminds me of a mortuary
with the bereaved moving back and forth
searching for the area
where their own are resting.
When they locate it,
they find only an empty room
with a name and emblem —
a diamond designating killed,
a cross signifying missing in action.
They tack flowers and notes and flags on the door
while the mothers and fathers
who bore the draft dodgers
wear their crosses
as they visit with their own
in rooms riddled with bullets of guilt
or papered with the peace sign
of the then familiar chicken foot design.

I glance at The Wall one last time
before The Wall moves to other cities.
Will it hasten a nation's healing process, as intended,
by neither glorifying war
nor condemning those who fought
in that unpopular call to arms,
when men and women on leave
were commanded to wear civilian clothes for their protection
then awarded the Medal of Honor
for conspicious gallantry beyond duty's call?

At the 200th Classic Coke Celebration,
will anyone remember The Wall?

EVE

Charles B. Dickson

He climbs, dejected, up the luminous slope,
eyes blind to autumn sunslant through the canopy
of crimson, gold and yellow leaves.
He had acted like a proper idiot, he thinks.
A year or more he had been struggling
to fortify his nerve enough to speak,
and he had spoken now, a stammer.

He still sees Susan's startled eyes,
the freckles on her nose. He sees her whirl
and race, squirrel-quick and graceful,
across the mountain schoolyard,
lustrous black braids tossing.
All he had asked was: Would she like
to go with him to pick a few ripe russets
in the abandoned orchard on the Turner farm?

He wonders if she abhors him so,
or is as shy as he. The forest ends.
The weedy orchard lies ahead. Something moves
beyond a sumac clump among the twisted trees.
He halts. A deer? A slender arm extends
above the bush to pluck an apple. A head appears.
He sees the sun-sheen on two thick, black braids.

PARENTAL GUIDANCE: RONNIE'S SECRET BOUQUET

Edward DeZurko

Pages of samples fanned past his face
smelling like cake batter. His scrubbed
hands, guided by a doting mother,
held a book too big for age seven
to manage alone without damage.
Gothic tracery, tartans of Scotland,
India prints, Buckingham guards . . .
a world of pattern to make a wall his own.
And he, flattered to make a choice,
his first really grown-up decision.

Then came the day for a red face.
Home from school, he raced to his room.
"Mom, what have you done! The wallpaper
is *not* bugles and ribbons!"
"Dear Ronnie, your choice is out of stock.
We would have to wait a long time to get it.
Isn't your new paper pretty?
Don't the violets look real?"
The boy muttered like, 'yes,' but
felt like, 'you broke your promise.'

The hurt childheart welcomed the day's end.
Bed: sleepless, hot, still as stone, weighing.
The need to remain silent kept
his thrashing in check. Past midnight,
with flashlight and penknife in hand
he scratched out, down to the raw paper,
one of the bunches of violets
on the wall out of sight, secreted
beneath his bed. The purple shreds
he threw at the night outside his window.

Weeks passed with much that bewildered him.
Visits. Kisses. Hushed voices running on.
Strange people coming in and out. Empty bed.
Strange reason for a mother to die, a
lump in the head. And Tante Ellen sorting
in mother's closet, and picking up
from the floor that scrap of wallpaper,

a bunch of violets, a shape cut just right
for his bruise. Ronnie asked for it;
no one knew why, not even Ronnie was sure.

But before he left to live with his father
he found some paste and made the patch . . .
crawling on hands and knees, penitent.

E. M. TANNER AWARD

SPONSOR: Anonymous

JUDGE: Tom Hendricks

FIRST: Ethelene Dyer Jones
Appalachian Farmer

SECOND: R. Riherd Greene
Hands On

THIRD: Patsy Anne Bickerstaff
Simon, the Maker of Bells

APPALACHIAN FARMER

Ethelene Dyer Jones

Bent from years at plow,
Overalls faded, hanging on a lanky frame,
He moves with deliberate plod
Following the faithful mare
On sloping hillside farm.

For generations the cycle has run:
He, dawn to dusk, determined
To wrest a living from the land,
Tills his acreage
And gathers what it yields.

The seasons turn, and weather, too,
Is friend or foe.
As fate would have it,
So be it.

He holds his own. He manages.
And no one tells him
What he has to do.

This freedom cloaks him more warmly
Than faded overalls and chambray shirt.

HANDS ON

R. Riherd Greene

Robin's egg sky and Mare's-tail clouds reflect
In windows forty, fifty stories high—
Architect's vision, booster's boast. But my eye
Turns back to rubble of buildings recently wrecked,

Bulldozers, smoky diesel dumps, back hoes,
Thumping pile driver, grumbling concrete trucks.
I recall the flare of acetylene, the flux
Of cladding over steel. I remember rows

And rows of partitions, clusters of wire and pipe.
Nor can I forget the men and women who swarm
The site to run machines and build each form,
Those who pause, with roughened hands, to wipe

Brows that are wet and red. Their grunts and yells,
The whine of sanders, the hum of drills still fret
My ears. I can sense cement dust mixed with body sweat,
Fresh sawn wood, acrylic and linseed smells.

Designer's thought and hope now wrought in steel
And glass—Chamber Of Commerce justly proud—
The working place for a bustling jostling crowd,
This "Work Of Art" belongs to rumpled jeans
And sunbronzed backs that bent to make it real.

SIMON, THE MAKER OF BELLS

Patsy Anne Bickerstaff

Some say there is more noble work with brass
Than making humble bells. I might have been
A craftsman in the palace of a king,
An artisan of temple ornaments
That show my skill, and tell the world my name.
But bells enchanted me for many years;
They fascinated me with form and tone,
Like metal birds that celebrated art
With melody and glitter when they moved.
The songs that bells play are the songs of life,
Strong sounds of working men and animals,
Sweet harmonies of field and marketplace.
Bells chant the coming of the caravan,
Of merchants, with their gems and colored rugs,
Their silks and magic spices, figs on strings.
Bells call the shepherds to their grazing sheep
And ring among the hills when sunset falls.
They jingle joyous laughter for a feast
Like sounds of stars, on dainty dancers' feet.
I never blushed to dedicate to God
The duties of a fashioner of bells,
The worthy task my hands have found to do.
It was the voice of bells that I heard first,
That sacred night when the Messiah came;
The tinkling bells of sheep that filled the street
As shepherds made their way to find the Child;
And in the stable's hush, the only sounds
Were tunkling from an ox that shook its head,
And jangle of some camels' harnesses,
As if the God of Israel ordained
Bell-music to be holiest of all,
As if wherever men proclaim God's love,
Rejoicing in His gifts to human kind,
Their song of joy should be the sound of bells.

AMALIE de LAUNAY THOMPSON AWARD

SPONSOR: Jannelle Jones McRee

JUDGE: Dr. Cecile G. Gray

FIRST: Memye Curtis Tucker

HONORABLE MENTION:

> Harriet Stovall Kelley
> **Cradle Stones**
>
> June Owens
> **In Lopsided Light**
>
> Dorothy Williamson Worth
> **The Blossoming**
>
> Connie J. Greene
> **Pawley's Island—To My Daughter**

LETTER TO MY COUSIN

Memye Curtis Tucker

Today again, a solo clarinet
brought the scent of your mother's shining floors
past polished banisters to me—eleven,
in the guest bed, listening to you

on your sleeping porch at midnight,
practicing. Into those summer
nights you played each phrase
over and over until it was perfect, Bach
a metronome of keys opening, closing,

blunt fingers, silver
rings snapped down over black.
Under the dotted halfs, sixteenth-notes,
syncopation—relentlessly keeping time,
was it your heel tapping,

or your toe? Send me this information.
Precision is the only way. Days
blur now before they are done. Sometimes
I find writing under a stack of papers,
and know it's mine only by the hand.

Are you still practicing? Who listens now,
tapping her heel, clapping her empty hands?
Be clear. Have you taught her French—
to give each syllable its separate beat,
accenting the last?

If your mother's gone, what lingers,
rising from the hardwood floors
that echoed every mistake, every perfection?
Have the notes rippled out past recall?

OUR HERITAGE POETRY AWARDS
Honoring Ethelene Dyer Jones

SPONSOR: G. Grayson Newman

JUDGE: Esther Alman

FIRST: Georgia T. Henry
Sins of Our Mothers

SECOND: Jeanne Osborne Shaw
The Trip Home

THIRD: Georgia T. Henry
The Dinner Bell

HONORABLE MENTION:

FIRST: Georgia T. Henry
Sins of the Fathers Revisit the Son

SECOND: Charles B. Dickson
Hands

THIRD: Louise Rogers
A Love of the Land

SINS OF THE MOTHER

Georgia T. Henry

My pen in hand provoked
the shocking thought,
"I need to write her"—my mother,
buried years ago, whom I never
wrote except to vent a seldom woe.
Startling that guilt engulfed me
after three decades plus. Is she
comforting me now to remind me
that my children, in their neglect
to keep in touch, remember me
as I remembered her
without token of script and fuss?
Will I visit them
after my living years grow dim
to offer my eternal presence
in their difficult desolation,
when their children turn
their backs and they are separated
from their own creation?

THE TRIP HOME

Jeanne Osborne Shaw

My father wanted to go back home,
back to the lapstrake mountains
holding up the glass roof of North Carolina.
He had been talking up the trip for three years,
but this fall his voice dropped an octave
and went through a tunnel of eighty-six years.
It was like when I had the measles
and, hiding his fatherly concern,
he was all doctor. "There now, you'll be better
tomorrow," he said, and I felt I had to be so.
So, taking him back to Brevard was a command.

My daughter and I drove him all around Highlands,
dropping down the cylinder to Horse Cove,
where, under a beaver dam of forests,
we saw the silver slabs bricking up
Whiteside Mountain—then to the bare hill
where the old home place once stood,
front porch aimed at the French Broad valley.

"Let's go see the old Osborne burial grounds,"
we suggested, thinking he might want to see graves
once more where father and grandfathers
gave names to waterfalls and mountains.
"Don't believe I want to," he declined meekly.
"Let's go to Mount Pisgah and Looking Glass Falls."
Into the dark thatched forest of balsams and firs
we rode slowly, sumac torches of welcome
waving us on. "We used to ride here in a sleigh,
pulled by horses through the snow," he said.
"It was good to have a girl beside you
and whisper little love things in her ear."
We stopped at the falls with their great shiny rock.
He stared for a long time. "What do you see, Doc?"
my daughter asked. "Perhaps myself,"
he replied softly. "My father and grandfathers
saw themselves here." We remembered the burial grounds
and wondered why he hadn't wanted to see them.

A month later, we understood.
"I'm glad we went to Looking Glass Falls,"
my daughter said as we stared at the tranquil face
in the foreign white hills of the casket.

THE DINNER BELL

Georgia T. Henry

PART I

How does a mother know
the feelings her child matches
to a place unless by some act
of what I call grace?
My son unknowingly told me
of his childhood happiness
when he reclaimed the black dinner bell
from our 1832-built Acworth house.
In his telling about discovering,
on a visit to the former homeplace,
the bell on its yoke,
the post fallen onto the now weed-covered bricks,
he lovingly recalled how he
and his two brothers and I
had dug the decaying rose-colored bricks
of an old apothecary out of the ground,
carefully laying each one to make a patio.
Not revealing our sadness at the empty closet
and my husband's note that prompted
their complicity in my obsession with physical labor
to ward off depression.
And how, in his talk with the owner,
twice tried to convince him of his need
to have the bell—
because "I lived here as a child."

Now moved from Georgia to front-door-prominence
at his Colorado address,
the bell in its yoke stands as a monument
to his childhood memories
and will be there,
drawing his children's attention
to its clear tolling ring,
a future reminder of their youthful pleasures
and concealed hurts.

Like my son, I hope their recollection
will persist with affection enough to rescue

that memento with the clapper
that called to that little boy
down that southern country road.

PART II

Holding close her eight month old Michelle,
I watch my son's wife walk down the
Colorado snow-covered steps
as she heads for the family dinner bell.

Curiously gazing at the black relic
erected outside their door over a year ago,
as though seeing it for the first time,
she examines this thing
which I had made the affectionate subject
of a rhyme celebrating my son's childhood.
As though the bell beckons her,
she repeatedly rings it
while her searching eyes speak to her child:
"Listen to the bell, Michelle,"
acknowledging her love for my son
and caring enough for me to
carry out the self-fulfilling prophecy
that would later tell of Michelle's happy youth
at the sight of the Mike Henry family bell.

EDWARD DAVIN VICKERS POETRY AWARD

SPONSOR: Major General and Mrs. Edmund C. Lynch

JUDGE: Margaret Boothe Baddour

WINNER: Bettie Sellers
Lament for an Old Bluejay

HONORABLE MENTION:

Thelma Hall
That August Morning

Charles B. Dickson
The Strength of Mountains

LAMENT FOR AN OLD BLUEJAY

Bettie Sellers

I watch you on my deck
pecking around the feeder,
sweeping sunflower seeds
into your blue-veined hands:
"I hate you pesky jays!
I will not let you eat!"

Your querulous tones echo
through the yard, scattering
my sparrows, chickadees,
and I would see you gone,
this visit suddenly overlong.

Once I could chuckle at your ways,
find eccentricities a charm.
Now, thinking you mean,
I crumble our bread, shred meats
grown rancid as this ancient tie:
"Old woman, I will not let *you* eat!"

I turn my back and hold my tongue
lest I should sound a raucous call,
see my fingers turning blue as yours.

GEORGIA STATE POETRY SOCIETY
ELEVENTH ANNIVERSARY AWARDS

CATEGORY I, TRADITIONAL

SPONSOR: Georgia State Poetry Society

JUDGE: Dr. John Vaughn

FIRST: Dorothy Williamson Worth
The Drought (Shakespearean Sonnet)

SECOND: Charles B. Dickson
Like Eagles We Would Spread Our Wings (Villanelle)

THIRD: Jeanne Osborne Shaw
To My Blue-Blocker Shades (Sonnet)

CATEGORY II, CONTEMPORARY FORM

JUDGE: Melba Dungey

FIRST: Angela Burns
Distant Side

SECOND: Thomas Theus
Transformation in Catchup

THIRD: William L. Davenport
Reflections on Being a Hero

HONORABLE MENTION:

FIRST: Dorothy Williamson Worth
Outside Eden

SECOND: R. Riherd Greene
Earthquake

THIRD: Georgia T. Henry
Greenwood Street

THE DROUGHT

Dorothy Williamson Worth

From May until the final amber shred
Of August moon had faded into dawn
It did not rain, until his land turned red
With blowing dust, and corn and grain were gone.

The cottonfields became a barren waste,
And in the dry creek bed his weary feet
Stirred only orange clouds that brought a taste
Of dying earth to signal his defeat.

He cursed and sweated through the endless days;
At night in restless dreams he heard the sound
Of raging rivers, saw a phantom maze
Of blood-red water cutting through the ground.

One morning, thunder rolled while he still slept:
He waked to rain on ruined crops, and wept.

LIKE EAGLES WE WOULD SPREAD OUR WINGS

Charles B. Dickson

The bright swans swam serenely on the lake.
We watched, young and vivacious, from the shore,
Unmindful that the future is opaque.

I vowed a life of triumph for your sake.
Like eagles we would spread our wings and soar.
The bright swans swam serenely on the lake.

No challenge was too great to undertake.
No obstacle could hinder us, I swore,
Unmindful that the future is opaque.

You, too, intrepid, pledged we would not quake
Whenever tempests flailed against our door.
The bright swans swam serenely on the lake.

Long years have tutored us in our mistake:
Youth cannot gauge the chastenings in store,
Unmindful that the future is opaque.

Yet, bruised and scarred, our spirits did not break.
Our love remains. We do not ask for more.
The bright swans swam serenely on the lake
Unmindful that the future is opaque.

TO MY BLUE-BLOCKER SHADES

Jeanne Osborne Shaw

Although you bring out gold in grasses, hay—
A Midas-touch that chemistry can bind
By diking out the blue and ultra ray
That makes my eyes opaque and stuns my mind,
The good you do is mostly by omission.
You prove, like pencils of non-photo blue,
That shortest light waves have the longest session
In spirits nourished by this planet's hue.
The blue of sky and sea, though delicate,
Has armored earth from gobbling black by day
And cold that fills our souls and habitat.
We live on light of hyacinth and jay.
  So, glasses, shield me only at high noon,
  Or joy is that to which I'm made immune.

DISTANT SIDE

Angela Burns

Progress
That makes an old man
Bent over his cane
Fearful when crossing
The country lane he remembers.

A twisted hand shades his cloudy eyes
As the stiff brown neck turns gingerly
Right—then left—then right again.
He creeps with caution onto the blue macadam.
Halfway across
A bright red blur
Whistles around the far corner.
The old one leans forward
—brittle rye in the wind—
And shuffle runs,
Connecting with the distant side.

Not minding death so much—
He fears expense and further pain.

TRANSFORMATION IN CATCHUP

Thomas Theus

It's June;
a friend and I are having dinner
at the Fifth Quarter
in Chattanooga
when a procession of elegantly-dressed
couples from one of the proms
files past us, taking tables;
their manners are courtly,
the princely tuxedos lustrous,
the silken, beautifully-feminine gowns
princess-like;
beverages and appetizers are served,
then steaks,
and all is regal.

Suddenly
one of the princesses
dressed in a lavender gown
of finest gossamer and satin, a maiden
who would not have seemed out of place
at the palace in Monaco
grabs a bottle of catchup
and shakes it vigorously over her plate,
finally splashing the stubborn red paste
over the steak and French fries.

Squinting against the lighting
which seems all at once strangely dim,
I watch in horror, helpless
as the princess is transformed
into a commoner
dressed in battered blue jeans,
a tee shirt bearing some gratuitous ad,
and smudged, car-like running shoes—
the uniform of the masses,
of followers,
of the world;
unbelievably
it is still nearly two hours until midnight.

REFLECTIONS ON BEING A HERO

William L. Davenport

It has long been my secret,
but you should know:
I am a hero—
rescuer of a lost child,

It wasn't in rugged mountains
or on a blistering desert,
but in a strange terrifying place
for a two-year-old lost from
family and friends.

Tiny arms squeezed my neck;
warm tears brushed my cheek;
sobs slowly subsided as I held
the little stranger in my arms.
He wanted his Mommie
but in his scary moment
I was a welcome surrogate.

I carried him up the steps
and returned him to his Mommie
after, unnoticed, he had strayed
from his Sunday school room,
out into the terrifying caverns
and forbidding cliffs
of a huge church building.

Well, maybe I'm not your classic hero.
But on a Sunday morning
a frightened two-year-old
let me know I was his hero—
a genuine hero.

1990 YOUTH POETRY COMPETITION WINNERS
Rebekah Stion, Chairman

Total entries for the 1990 GSPS Youth Awards in Poetry were 1,705. Every student submitting a poem is to be commended. Just to enter is an accomplishment within itself. Winners are listed below. Each winner has been notified and received a certificate of commendation. First, second and third place winners also received a monetary award.

ELEMENTARY SCHOOL (Grades 1–4)
Total Student Entries: 768

FIRST: Elisa Dallas, Eastside Elementary, Senoia, "Bubbles, Like Little Glass Homes"

SECOND: Preston Wilkinson, Elcan-King Elementary, Bainbridge, "The Rose in My Heart"

THIRD: David Issa, Austin School, Dunwoody, "Math"

HONORABLE MENTIONS (In Alphabetical Order):
Nikki Ancrum, Hickory Hills School, Marietta, "Ode to My Eyes"
Monique Jenkins, Northside Elementary, Cairo, "You"
Dean Klear, St. Simons Elementary, St. Simons Island, "Blue Whales"
Kyle Martin, Northside School, Albany, "Speckled and Freckled"
Amanda Owen, Powder Springs Elementary, Powder Springs, "Raindrops"
Pamela Walls, Southwestern Elementary, Cordele, "The Squirrel"
Mindy Ward, Central Elementary, Dublin, "The New Chickens"

MIDDLE SCHOOL (Grades 5–8)
Total Student Entries: 815

FIRST: Kirt Ertzberger, Telfair County Middle, McRae, "Life"

SECOND: Margaret Rich, Brookwood School, Thomasville, "Villanelle: Dream Flight"

THIRD: Sara Zuk, Tritt Elementary, Marietta, "If My Ears Could Listen"

HONORABLE MENTIONS (In Alphabetical Order):
  Dehanza Rogers, Eddy Junior High, Columbus, "Martin Luther King and His Dream"
  Edgardo Garcia, Riverdale Elementary, Riverdale, "As"
  Stephanie M. Keating, Renfroe Middle School, Decatur, "Grasping an Illusion"
  Patrick Reynolds, St. Thomas More School, Decatur, "Innercomputer Hero"
  Carole Van Sickle, Barnett Shoals Elementary School, Athens, "I Am a Dogwood"
  Ann Tapp, Menlo Elementary School, Menlo, "If I Were a Trainer"
  Courtney Zep, Haynes Bridge Middle School, Alpharetta, "Come Set Ya Down on the Porch"

HIGH SCHOOL (Grades 9–12)
Total Student Entries: 122

FIRST: Matthew Thompson, Monroe High School, Monroe, "Quilts"

SECOND: Lori Barfield, Brunswick High School, Brunswick, "Portrait of Gaute"

THIRD: Paige Haggard, Northside High School, Warner Robins, "Patterned Dance"

HONORABLE MENTIONS (In Alphabetical Order):
  Beatriz Alvarado, St. Pius X High School, Atlanta, "The Neglected"
  Edward Barnsley, St. Pius X High School, Atlanta, "Calculus"
  Christine Deaton, Darlington School, Rome, "How Well My Flesh"
  Andrew Hancock, Columbus High School, Columbus, "Opposing Voices"
  Andrew Oyefesobi, Riverdale Junior High School, Riverdale, "The Art of Dreaming"
  Kimberly C. Parker, Stewart Quitman High School, Lumpkin, "Who Can Save Us?"
  Kathryn Stine, Henderson High School, Chamblee, "An English Sonnet"

BUBBLES—LIKE LITTLE GLASS HOMES

Elisa Dallas

Bubbles,
Like little glass homes
That fall from the sky,
With little men,
Women,
And children,
That go drifting by.
You can look in
And see a kind face,
But when the bubbles burst
They must find a new place.
The little children,
Smiling so bright,
I wish I would dream of them,
In the deep dark night.
But when they reach up
To shake your hand,
They fall apart like castles,
Made of sand.
But now they are gone,
They've all burst and died,
I'll just have to make more
To drift by my side.
And I wish that the next ones
Would come and be mine,
Those little glass homes
So wonderfully fine.

THE ROSE IN MY HEART

Preston Wilkinson

The Rose in my heart
Sheds spirit into my life.
Its bright red color
Is only part of its beauty,
Its existence is hardly ever
   recognized.
But, when my heart breaks
There it is, sticking its thorns
   into me
Like a knife of anguish and despair,
But I know it will pass.
My heart—its Rose
   are a great pair.

MATH

David Issa

Math is like a game to me;
The numbers are my friends, you see.
I add them up and take some away,
Multiply others and divide some for play.

I use them to measure distance or shape,
For shopping or cooking they work out just great.
Using math in my life every day,
Makes me think it's a game for everyone to play.

LIFE

Bradley Kirk Ertzberger

Life is like a single thread,
So delicate.
Life can come in a variety of colors.
You can choose which one you want.
Life can come in many lengths.
You may have a spool of your own.

You may be sewn, along with others,
Into the quilt of the world.
You and God alone
Can choose the stitch of your thread.
We are each a skein
In the workbasket of life.

VILLANELLE: DREAM FLIGHT

Margaret Rich

I'd like to see snow geese take flight
Before the fall of the first snowflake,
With their graceful bodies of pure white.

Flying with them I'd have no fright,
Calmly I'd rise from the freezing lake,
I'd like to see snow geese take flight.

I'd try to keep them in my sight,
And map the route that they would take,
With their graceful bodies of pure white.

I'd rise to an amazing height,
It would be so cold that I would shake,
I'd like to see snow geese take flight.

I'd soar with them all through the night,
Never leaving the formation they make,
With their graceful bodies of pure white.

At last I'd feel warm southern light—
But to the cold I would awake.
I'd like to see snow geese take flight
With their graceful bodies of pure white.

IF MY EARS COULD LISTEN

Sara Zuk

If my ears could listen,
I could hear the cotton ball
drop,
Falling from my fingers
To hit the floor below.
If my ears could listen,
I could meet that butterfly,
Meet him ear to ear
Instead of eye to eye.
I could hear the dust
Rubbing off
Those delicate little wings,
Just the kind of thing I'd
like to do.
If my ears could listen,
I could hear myself begin to
wonder
If birds really make music,
As I have seen some say.
And most of all,
I'd like to translate the sound
of nothing.
That stale, dead sound of nothing
Nesting in my ears, day after day.
Oh, if my ears could listen,
I could hear the sound
Of frustration in my throat,
Now that I finally understand
That I
Am deaf.

QUILTS

Matthew Thompson

they were just meant as covers in winter
as weapons
against pounding January winds

but it was just that every morning I awoke to these
october ripened canvases
passed my hand across their faces
and began to wonder how you pieced
all this together

these strips of gentle cotton and flannel nightgowns
old clothes and dime store cloth

how you shaped patterns square and oblong and round
positioned
balanced
then cemented them
with your thread darting in and out
galloping along the frayed edges, tucking them in
as you did us at night

in the evening you sat at your canvas
-our cracked linoleum floor the drawing board
me lounging on your arm
and staking out the plan:
whether to put the lilac purple of easter against the red
plaid of winter
whether to mix a yellow with a blue
whether to shape a five-point star from
the somber black silk you wore to grandfather's funeral

you were the river current
carrying the roaring notes
forming them into pictures of a little boy's dreams
sewn hard and taut to withstand the trashing of 50 years
stretched out they lay
armed, ready, shouting, celebrating

knotted with love
the quilts sing on.

PORTRAIT OF GAUTE

Lori Barfield

Just sort of sitting there
doodling a Norwegian doodle
on a blank sheet . . .

Deep in thought, he has been
Westernized—to a certain extent.
A "Year of the Pirates" button
dangles from his sweater
while an exquisite Swedish timepiece of
silver and gold encircles his wrist.

Incredible blue eyes,
so indescribably alive
with charm and sincerity,
gaze at the teacher with courteous interest.

In an instant
his thought pattern is broken and
a somber yawn escapes,
silently downplaying our
imagined differences.

---

*Gaute is a Norwegian exchange student who is studying at Brunswick High School.

107

PATTERNED DANCE

Paige Haggard

We dance a patterned dance.
    With elaborate steps,
    we waltz in and out of others'
        lives, ever retaining
    our form, always keeping
        our space.
    Twirling around
        one person,
        swirling away
            from another—
Never getting closer to another
        than the past will allow.
    We keep the band playing
        the same waltz
        over again,
        never altering the beat.
But there are more
        galliards than this,
    More jigs that can be done.
    Do we not each hear,
        in the corners of our minds,
    a hauntingly beautiful strain,
        different from the original?

So dance to your music
        whether it is a stately
            waltz or vivacious jig,
    and fear not that another
        may not hear what you do
            or move as you will,
                for the price of dancing
                    as does the rest
        of the ballroom when
                you are your own conductor
            is far greater than the
                price of dancing
                your own measure.

108

Though you may be alone,
you will be adding
      to the beauty
of the minuet
            called Life.

MEMBER POEMS

A MEMORY I KEEP

JoAnn Yeager Adkins

It is summer, and he is two.
Mother, the Dodge full of children,
   all young and laughing siblings,
carefully urges the big car over weed-grown ruts.
I carry him from the car, down the steep bank,
over the rocky high water line to the shore—
carry him on my shoulders,
     little bare legs and feet under my chin,
     chubby fingers wound into my hair.
     I am sixteen, and he is my brother.
                    He is my love.
Mother spreads a blanket;
         I put the baby on his feet.

Like a killdeer he runs
        down the slope
              into the water.
Before my eyes, before I can think,
      he runs into the swiftly flowing river
               and is gone.
I fly to the water,
         take its icy shock as I go deep,
See his white body and pale hair
            rolling in the current.
Sand roils from the bottom of the river;
           the water is dark—
I struggle to see, hold my breath, swim faster—
he washes ahead of me, sliding
          deeper into the channel.

I am crazy with fear—I am **wild** with fear.
 I seize him at the waist,
    clutch his white birdseye diaper—
      lunge toward the steep and rocky bank,
         far downstream from where we were.

A choking, laughing child
  wraps about my neck again,
        repeating my name . . .
"Jo Jo, Jo Jo," still holding on to my hair.

AUSTIN'S MILL—1785
(Austin's Creek at the Conneross)
To Nathan Austin, Jr.

Aurelia Austin

In fall
Nat Austin's mill turns full gait . . .
The wheel sings Manning . . . Manning . . . Manning;
Sweet kernels turn to gold, while rice birds sing,
And fragrant hogsheads catch the meal . . .
The crows fly down . . . never late . . .
To eat their fill with crow-like zeal,
While robins watch from tops of trees and wait.

In wintertime
His crystal creek is solid ice
And Austin's mill no longer whispers
Manning . . . Manning . . . Manning; the dark green firs
Are locked in snow; his wagon makes
Its blue-white tracks. It will suffice
To heap the fires . . . where cornbread bakes
In shucks . . . and doves lie brown on beds of rice.

Note: Conneross Creek flows into the Keowee River near the South Carolina/Georgia line, now Oconee County, formerly Pendleton County. According to Colonial custom, Nathan, Jr. named his first-born son **Walter Manning Austin** for an ancestor.

ON WRITING POETRY TO SAVE MY LIFE

D. Heather Ballew

My eloquence has been retired for far too long.

But this unbearable field of icy spikes and heartache
Has caused me to call forth my pen and write.
Can the flowing of ink calm the flowing of pain?
Can I ever sleep in love or hope again?
Can I ever thaw this glacier of pain?
Will my love ever come again?

THE SMELL OF BOXWOOD

Frances L. Barber

What makes a magic spell?
Is it the smell of boxwood,
So tall and green, shrub after shrub
Head high and level with my nose?

Or is it the sound of walking on pea gravel?
Could it be the shine
Of early light on clapboard walls?

Maybe the pleasure is caused
By the sight of so many old trees.
Magnolia, cedar.
Just the sound of naming sugar hackberry
Is delicious.

If the joy is not these
Then perhaps it is the sight of Cornelia's garden.
Secluded with small statue and iron bench
All shaded and cool.

The truth is, it is all these,
And his presence so close to my left side
As he holds the paper
While I do the rubbing with waxed pencil:

The National Register of Historic Places
South Carolina
Fort
Hill.

A CURIOUS INTIMACY WITH HOPE

Mildred Barthel

For years
the whip was taken from
darkened corner of the room
to employ obedience to his youth.

His body obeyed.
His seeking mind
refused counterfeit power.
Isolated in his room after each infraction
he found release from stinging pain
watching wisps and swirls of clouds
winging escape across the sky beyond his window.

Escape became ritual and curious intimacy
with sun-covered mists and haze
with night moon only partially obscured
                    by winter puffed with ice
with slanted rain
                    not daring to argue the storm.
Sketches filled notebooks
and became paintings of sky glorified.
Angles and design—
pigment of an upturned face.

OPENING DAY

Richard G. Beyer

Lost in a labyrinth of flowcharts, machine halts,
Unwritten programs, and a host of irate users . . .
Confounded in a conspiracy of crab grass,
Overdue library books, and mortgage payments
That escalate like blood pressure . . .
Bogged down here in middle age, overweight,
Mature only in portly appearance . . .
Here, incredibly, the first day of trout season
Passes unnoticed . . . unthought . . . unfished . . .
Again and again, for year after year.
Where now are the mists that burned off the streams
Like dreams that ended a long sleepless night?
Where now are the days that floated up to the sun
In a circle of gulp from rising expectations?
Where now the quiver of anticipation, the throb
In the blood that said not just alive, but living?
And where the imported fly rod, the delicate cast,
The tapered presentation of such sweet temptation,
The cool waters stocked with speckled surprises
And the dreams so deep it took hip boots to cross?

THE GRASS IS GREENER . . . .

Jeffrey H. Biggers

In the middle of nowhere
Everywhere you look
  is somewhere

Should e'er you go somewhere
You might look back
  at nowhere

There you'll see a somewhere
And wish that you were
  still there

Go on back to somewhere
And love what brings you
  back there!

IN THESE AUTUMN DAYS

Marel Brown

Somehow in these autumn days I lost
My fear of growing old,
Watching the beauty of a world
Triumphantly change to gold,
Hearing exultant cries transformed
To rustling overtones,
Tasting the richness of wild grapes
A frosty finger owns;
Feeling the final warmth, the peace
That autumns calmly bring:
Somehow I know that age can be
A brave and lovely thing.

REPROOF

Archie Buie

I woke up alone in my bed
sleeping a healer into my head,
I did not want my hurt to get
so warm
I could not find rest without it.

So I took to my feet
in a sunny time to figure
just what happiness has to do
with the sweet vapors of
a solitary cloud,
just what my smiling might
do to tone up soft green grass
and grave, silent trees.

Finally, many pains ago I decided
not to work at it so hard
since I got along as well
one way as another.

Then I viewed the hurt and the joy
as sister and brother
both siblings of a family
that dented me in youth
but, for which,
by now,
I have no reproof.

MEMORIAL DAY

Angela Burns

I miss sitting on the graves
  Eating chocolate cake
    And deviled eggs
      And drumsticks.
Well deserved, too—after all that raking.
The town came to the cemetery
  On that special day.
Families cleaned their plots.
Flowers, soon dead as the occupants,
Were placed on every grave.
  And when the food was spread
    We ate with loved ones—
      Quick and dead.
I usually sat on Grandpapa,
And wondered if he knew I was there,
Thinking—maybe they came out at night
  And looked around
    Happy to see
      Someone still cared.
Glad they didn't come while I was there
Didn't want to see hair and fingernails
  That never ceased to grow,
Or battle wounds that never healed.
Perpetual care takes all the fun away
And leaves but one more party week-end
  Beer cans left to witness
    And lists of highway deaths
      To scan.
I miss sitting on my grandpa's grave
  Eating chocolate cake
    And deviled eggs
      And drumsticks.

ARBELIAS'S FAREWELL

Ernest Camp, Jr.

Goodbye, Arbelias—
adored by butterflies and men,
queen of our waking Midsummer Day's Dream.

I float in fragrance through the drowsy hours . . .
Where other stimuli fall down,
  you send me soaring.
Your fantasy feeds my senses well . . .
Enchantress, come again and weave your spell.

Prisoner of your possessive perfume,
I walk in wonder at your magic mixture,
ethereal, tender femininity
with Eve's raw, earth power.

You orchestrate a silent chorus of voices
I surrender to sensuous revery.
In memory—I see geraniums
  blazing red against a leafy-green.
I hear a Horowitz piano concerto
Serenade a sky full of stars.

I taste champagne . . .
catching the gleam of firelight.
I feel slim fingers tugging at my arm
I sway to a waltz that says,
"You're falling in love."

I vibrate to a kiss
  that sets all my senses on fire
I glimpse a shapely ankle
  that twinkles when she walks
Your fantasy feeds my senses well . . .
Enchantress, come again and weave your spell!

ORNAMENTS

Patricia E. Canterbury

The kid wore
5 multicoloured
bracelets around his
left wrist
cloth, ragged bits
of twine and wool,
a single silver band
which caught the light
as he wrote.
Copper healers
clasp tightly flashing
tarnished colours on the pages
of his book
and finally a wide
black, leather band
studded with tiny
silver pyramids
encircling a
Mickey Mouse-faced
watch.

CAMPUS ENCOUNTER

Margery Carlson

She lay curled in lilac's shade
Like a tiny splash of winter's hidden snow
Left when spring sunshine melts the quilt
Of flakes to help the gardens grow.

I prr-meowed a friendly greeting,
Inviting brief conversation.
She woke, stretched, yawned, and stood,
Identifying my location.

I prr-meowed again, with more response—
A purring fluff of white
Sashayed across the grass to me
And prr-meowed feline delight,

We sat together, cat and I;
She rubbed against my hand.
I scratched her ears, her neck, her chin—
Joy more than cat can stand!

We talked and purred, white cat and I.
She curled up on my lap
Until I had to leave for class
And she resumed her nap.

SPIDER WEAVERS

Wil Carter

In the trees I see them,
spiders dancing on autumn winds,
weaving the last wispy strands
of honey summer
into shrouds for memories.
 In my dreams I see them,
 patiently spinning, spinning,
 casting wide their silky nets
 of fine knit lace
 for all that flutters or flies,
  fishing deep the rushing air
  for moths and stars
  and human souls.

ETERNITY'S EDGE

Mary Chase

I am a mind wanderer
A dream builder
A star gazer.

I jostle for space with atoms
Pull ideas apart
And muse on their core of conception.

I chase rainbows with unicorns
Expand fantasies
And leap beyond the impossible.

I raise monoliths of words
Set rhymes in motion
Build monuments of form.

I reach the edge of time
Stretching so far
My world tilts toward eternity.

HER KIND OF MUSIC

Mary F. Childs

Today she wears her faces like Janus.
Evenings, does English courses to
polish prose for writing her novel.
Afternoons, tunes in to FM for the big band
sounds—she loves the music and the lyrics
of Glen Miller, Tommy Dorsey, Dick Haymes,
Doris Day. . . .

The emptiness of every space is filled.
The rhythm rolls back time to when
she was young and lovely, and he was there
to share the meaning in the songs.

The music reaches in and awakens something
that should have been long gone. She feels
the way it gives her heart a squeeze and
weighs her down like loneliness.
Memories, full of intimate patterns,
cut through her like a longing
that adolescents feel wanting to be grownup.

To her locked away past, this hour
of music is the key
she never threw away.

The station announces the "return to our
regular programming" as though it had come
from another world, and the room returns
to her present. She switches to news
and cannot take time to remember
that she also knows some blues tunes.

THE HOUNDED WIND

Jerome A. Connor

The hounded wind sweeping over the hill
In wild raucous groans hideous and shrill
Yawning and yapping in forceful rushes
Dashing madly in destructive gushes
   It came—and the night was dark.

Carelessly hastening in a blundering way
Finding no place where it wanted to stay
Failing to heed rugged hands in the air
Beckoned by nature to stop here and there
   It came—and the night was dark.

With speed advancing its reckless race
Moaning loud from its hazardous pace
Closer it bent itself to the ground
Harder it ran with ravenous sounds
   It came—and the night was dark.

Hours passed by and the wind traveled on
Pressing its race toward the break of dawn
From hills to lowland in dashing sprints
Leaving tracks of indelible prints
   It came—and the dawn was near.

Making its way toward the angry sea
'Twas something it did quite naturally
The hounded wind made its last great stride
But the strain was heavy against the tide
   And it crashed—as the dawn appeared.

GOD'S EARTH

Della Martin Cook

The water reflects the forest green,
The silhouette of deer are seen.
The soft white clouds where eagles fly,
A waterfall splashes nearby.

I walk by a bubbling stream and see
The rainbow trout floating so free.
The sun reflects the water there
As I pause and say a silent prayer.

Of God's green earth and heaven blue,
Man can see the tree that grew
From an acorn and he might have learned
Nature's secrets and be concerned.

For scenes like these are very rare—
City builders do not care.
Of God and Nature they give no heed,
Thinking only of their greed.

This old earth may soon pass away,
Nature is in disarray
With dirty water, polluted air,
Surely we must show more care.

WATCHING TIME GROW OLD

Charles E. Cravey

The ivy that clings to the vine has loosed its grip
And now turns faded gray with winter's eve.
I watch the flocks of birds as they pass my window
on their southerly flight.
One seems to tag along behind, reluctantly,
Refusing to go—rejecting what lies ahead—
Forsaking time and its calling to "Press On."
My spirit bleeds for that small fowl who
fights against the prevailing winds and that
compelling force which will carry it from its home
to some resting-station for a season.
Life will have changed when he makes the flight
northward again.
Things will never be the same.
Age will have again taken its toll,
As one watches time grow old.

I am not the same today as yesterday.
Feelings of joy, sorrow, pain and grief
Have all compassed my soul,
Creating that which I am today.
I seek the past again to some
simpler, joyous time—but it evades me
and reminds me to "Press On."
As I sit by these memories and feel the bitter cold—
I rest in my labors
While watching time grow old.

GLOBAL WARMING

Gerry Crocker

I felt the sun's warmth against my face
And suddenly the whole human race
Sprang into view.

Is man following nature's calling?
Does he feel that global warming
Will melt icy hearts anew?

Hot cries of "freedom" fill the air
And everywhere
Walls are felled and bars of iron
Break with an exultant clatter
As men's hearts are heated by high hopes
And their righteous goals are all that matter.

PUTTING ASUNDER

William L. Davenport

The first thing she noticed
was how high the judge sits,
as if the common law
requires petitioners be made aware
of their insignificance—
a fact confirmed
by the droning voice of the clerk
recounting what has happened
countless times before,
will happen countless times again.

Her name is read in monotone—
given name, maiden name, married name;
followed by a sing-song recitation
of reasons, made precisely vague,
for this marriage to be dissolved
by the grinding machinery of The State.

The robed figure huddles
with hovering hirelings.
All agree—the papers
are in order. A pen affixes
today's strange words of severance
to yesterday's
familiar names of alliance.
No one sheds a tear;
no one offers back seven years.

"All rise." The judge steps down—
only half-way down to the level
where the insignificant ones stand—
to swish through a mammoth door,
as he has countless times before,
will do countless times again,
after freeing Petitioner and Respondent
from the burden
of punishing each other
for their differences.

GROWING OLD

Beverly Denmark

So what if my hair is gray?
It is only that way because
of havin' gone through both
the bitter and spicey taste
    of life.

So what if I walk with a cane.
It is only because of havin'
walked with the grace 'n' poise
of bein' an attractive young
lady. My how times change!

I may have wrinkles, but it is
only the reminder of the charmin'
smiles that I have given in my life.

And, what if my eyes are growin' dim, for
this is due to the years of examin' and
lookin' at the world through God's eyes
    instead of man's.

And my voice might not have the
glorious pitch as it once did, due
to the years of singin' 'n' praisin'
the Lord. His grace is sufficient!

Age 'n' growin' physically old may
be hard for you, but not for me.
Physical features are what you make
them out to be and I say that the Lord
has made me the way I am to be.
Love 'n' everlasting peace with God
is all that matters to me.

MARRIED PEOPLE

Delores Denmark

They say that married people
don't talk to each other, much.
Talk isn't always words
flowing from the mouth, spoken words.
True talk includes emotion,
attitude, attention, surrender,
a deep abiding love.
I sat across the table
from my beloved.
He smiled, I winked.
He looked into my eyes, my eyes sparkled.
We felt togetherness, a bonding.
We talked, but not a word was spoken.
So, married people do talk.

STREET PEOPLE

Herbert Walter Denmark

They continue to come.
All seem to look alike,
but all are different.
They come,
these people of the street,
from somewhere,
headed to nowhere,
looking for some care.
They have a stoic expression
on their faces.
Their eyes look,
but do not seem to see.
The lines in their faces
tell their personal story.
Their gaits suggest
there is no specific destination
to reach.
They continue to come.
In the past they all looked alike.
But now, some are distinctively different.
That difference is the stomach-wrenching,
small, sad-eyed faces of children.

ELEGY FOR A MOUNTAIN POET
(To Byron Herbert Reece)

Charles B. Dickson

Blue mountains leaning on the sky
Were grist to feed his Orphic mill.
  His word-lute rang
With wood thrush fluting, nighthawk cry,
With thump of spry square-dance quadrille.
  His stanzas sang
Of speckled wrens and coteries
Of minnows, dragonflies and bees,
Of foxes, deer sprawled at their ease
In laurel thickets; yes, from these
  His ballads sprang.

He heard the chords of lilting looms
That weave both bridal veil and shroud.
  He knew time guides
All human flesh to musty tombs.
Both life and death were fields he plowed.
  His verse confides
A wisdom many cannot see:
Existence is one tapestry
Of universal majesty,
The star, the human brain, the tree.
  This truth abides.

THANK YOU, LORD

Nelle Branan Ennis

I thank you, God, for blessings, ever present in my life—
The abiding good so evident, despite prevailing strife—
The sunshine and the rainfall, the wind's pervasive cool,
The rainbow hues to marvel at in each reflecting pool.

Thank you for my precious home, the comfort of my chair—
The bed that offers welcome and allows relief from care—
The kitchen where I go to cook the food that keeps us strong,
And loved ones who indulge me with the wants for which I long.

I'm grateful, Father, for the will to fill some other's need—
To do a little extra, and sow a kindness seed . . .
For joy of bringing pleasure into someone's world of woe,
And giving just a word of hope to help the sadness go.

For nature's green, to soothe the eyes, when they are
    drained of tears—
For busy obligations that help dull my selfish fears—
Your faithful ear, each time I pray, for daily health and rest—
In countless ways, I thank you, Lord . . . In all these things,
    I'm blessed.

ANTAGONIST

C. Russell Farmer

Writing this poem has become a disaster.
I am the slave and it is the master.
I pound out the phrases, I tune-up the tone,
But this wicked poem has a mind of its own.

I change it, arrange it, and pray for a rhyme.
It stares back at me like a smirk on a mime.
I tell it, I yell it, "Fit here, some damn word!"
But just as it's forming, it flits like a bird.

My head is now hanging; my chin on my chest.
My breathing is shallow. My mood is depressed.
My left hand is twitching. My right hand is numb.
The poem . . . it has won . . . and I will succumb.

So, this is "our" entry. This is our best.
Please consider these verses in your next contest.
In spite of my travail, if this poem's a winner,
Award not this poet . . . award my tormenter.

BURIAL OF A FIREMAN
For Alex Bealer

Neil L. Fraser

Just after the graveside service
I heard the mourning of engines.
A ladder truck and two pumpers
trailed by sirens now without
the urgency of midnight
or the stirring of fears
which run as deep as the beds
where coffins lie at rest.

The big machines are once again
the toys of a growing boy,
And I think of the joy he always held
in the flashing of their lights,
the reflections of red on polished chrome.

WHEN BABY SLEEPS

B. I. Garland

When baby sleeps, an angel sings;
It hovers o'er his tiny crib on gossamer wings,
When baby sleeps.

And deep inside his tousled head
He hears the words the cherubs said,
When baby sleeps.

Ah, sleep, my little one, and so
To dream, my baby, and to grow,
In baby sleep.

Smile on, my sweet, and listen sharp
To hear the strains from heaven's harp
That come to you, as baby sleeps.

Be still, harsh world; be still and let
The peace of heaven's magic net
Fall o'er us all, as baby sleeps.

CASTING

Betty Lou Gore

The moon
      casts
            its
                  light
upon the sea
as a fisherman
      casts
            a
                  net,
gathers
irridescent moonbeams,
      sets
            them
                  sailing
on the rim
of the waves.

WISTERIA

Mildred Greear

Wisteria is the color of its wistful name;
Not nearly purple; hardly lavender—

It smells that same luminous pale;
The smell, more provocative than real
Of crepe paper costumes we wore;
Skirts made from clumsily shaped leaves,
With festoons of crinkly blossoms, burgeoning,
Three dimensional as our mothers could make;
Costumes as much on trial as the performers
In Fourth Grade Spring Festival.

One must be careful in the wisteria dance;
The basting stitches might tear through
And a petal fall to the gymnasium stage floor

The way the March wind breaks
The thread holding wisteria clusters
In the top of the captive pine
To spatter occasional soft color,
Crepe paper smell, by the kitchen door.

SONG FOR SPRING

Connie J. Green

While peas
  swell and pop
    we eat—

Lettuce, radishes
  broccoli
    and spinach.

Drunk at the feast
  we plant
    for summer

Our backs
  bent
    to earth and sun.

All winter we'll eat
  tomatoes
    green beans

And if we must
  squash
    squash
      and squash.

ECSTACY

Lt. James L. Green

A man can soar on mental wings
To heights of ecstasy.
The mountains and the valleys fall away
As winged thoughts approach the clouds.

The sun sets, the moon rises
And a man's dreams fluctuate.
Now like the magnificent Bald Eagle
Man glides over his encompassed universe.

SANDSPUR SINGS HIS HERO

R. Riherd Greene

In awe, we all stood back.
His wooly head rose high
Above the rest; from there
He kept his watch with an eye
That weighed everything going on.
Both staunch and daring, he gave
Himself, held nothing back.
His spiny leaves would wave
Undaunted by drought or deluge.
His buoyant seed have spread
All over our sandy plain
And beyond; so everyone said
He was tops as family head.
His stalk grew tall to spend
His days cavorting with clouds
And nights at a ball with stars.
His winning deeds were ours,
His trophies ours as well,
His defeat occasion for grief.
We'll never be able to expel
The void that gnaws our ribs.
He was a Tower, a Prince;
We lag for lack of his like
To inspire our dreams ever since
That rattling, rocking mowing
Machine came snapping around
And laid our Paradigm,
The Thistle, flat on the ground!

IN ROUSSEAU'S GARDEN

Anthony Grooms

A red sun hangs
Over the black, verdant jungle.
Beneath the towering cycads,
Among the lotus blossoms, the sansevierias and the agave,
Between the columns of flowering cereus,
An ocelot attacks my silhouette.

I never expected
That my death would come even before I was born,
Dreamt of by a Frenchman
And sold for money.

I have memories of its coming,
Of time flowing backwards like an eddy.
Rousseau caught it in his strokes:
Feline, *feline of the yellow fang*
And me, running like the twilight,
From the thing the artist knows.

IN WORD

Janet A. Habas

Some softer
shadow
seeks - our
sacred - hardened
ground --- we've
fenced the open
plain - of
unique
thought - barbed
wire -- staked
plots - guarded
boundaries ---
killed -- to
keep change
out -----.
Space - we've
altered - to
eke - our
pleasures
stifles - under
refuse - persuasion
wrought - it
was the
narrowing
circle -
persistence - forced
there is
no out ---.
Some safer
day - we'll
turn the
inward 'round -
flip - off the
canopy - undo the
lace - we've
pulled - so taut --
freedom - it's
what
we - fought.

THE HAND PRINT

Wilson Hall

I've heard your awed and silent cry, Cousin,
Across unnumbered centuries dim grown,
Your palm print soft in ochre blown
Against the dull cave wall in Gargas' glen.
The self inside you leapt to be unfrozen
To say "I am" upon the timeless stone.
You left your mark of mind—not bone alone.
I feel your fossil joy conveyed therein.

It wasn't much to palm a wall and blow
A silhouetted hand in dust outlined.
But that prime effort did on Man bestow
The poet's mind, new and unrefined,
And cast the way that inward man must plod
Himself to light—to stand in the image of God.

COVECREST

Maxine Hamm

There is a country of luxury.
Where birds have pulpits on top of the trees
And the chorus sings beneath their shelf wings
As water takes bruises and moves with ease
Into nature that spares its earth nothing.

There is a country of luxury.
Where the light will flutter in the valley
Climbing in the windows between the trees
Like messengers taking light to the hills
And the wind gathers voices as it wills.

There is a country of luxury.
The valley bonded in soil of the past
Hills are veined in radiance of the present
The sun hot with play spreads its umbrella
Trying to tease the trees idling in air.

There is a country of luxury.
Where the mind is pastured out ankle-deep
Where the sound and silence will sing as one
As we rehearse and the air fills our lungs,
With a cool abundance of what gives life.

TREASURES

Elizabeth Ann Hammill

Old man ocean - grant me a treasure,
a gift of love from the sea;
a token to offer to my Beloved
when I make my anxious plea.

A pearl from the deep, if you've one to spare;
or a perfect, beautiful shell;
perhaps a piece of ocean glass
with the secrets it could tell.

Or even a shell that's broken,
and tossed by the sand and sea
'til it's polished as smooth as a jeweled stone,
would be a gift for me.

Old man ocean - grant me a treasure,
a beautiful gift from the sea;
something to give my loved one pleasure
while she hears my anxious plea.

I WANTED TO GO HOME AGAIN

Barbara Harris Harper

Go back to places I had gone,
Do again the things I had done,
Renew old friendships. Laugh. And weep.
Kindle old loves—fires long asleep.

I walked through the familiar land;
And did the things that I had planned.
A lesson learned—and one to share—
I was home. But HOME was not there.

HOME is not something here,
Nor something left behind.
HOME is—a state of mind.

NIGHT STALKER

Mavis H. Harrell

The golden topaz glow
  of some small creature's eyes
Flares in the headlights
  on a moonless night.

Like twin targets
  at the shooting gallery
  of a county fair,
The blazing orbs
  swing across the ebonscape
And disappear.

The sudden screech of a ground bird
  pierces the quiet,
Then silence closes in
  like the black waters
  of a cypress swamp
After the 'gator's passing.

THE SPIRITUAL DESERT

Jane L. Hart

Where has the music gone?
That love and sweetness
Goodness and delight.
The days run cold
And touch me not,
For I have wept in silence
Forlorn, seeing naught
But endless time
Day after day
No notes of comfort
Come to lift the weight
From off my heart.
Where has the music gone?

SOLSTICE SOLACE

Susan Harvey

Beautiful Wise Women:

In ancient greeting we
massage mutual wing roots.

Our eyes console
the loneliness of
angel fatigue.

"IN MONTEGO BAY"

Beverly V. Head

in montego bay
waves suck at the
rocky beach while
the hotel retreats
behind the patio

on the road
black women cluster
like colorful parrots
red and green rags cresting
their cornrowed hair
as they chirp and chatter
about the fruit and bamboo

one cuts a pineapple
and another asks to trade
for my sister's jogging shoes

from the patio
we watch the shacks
press against each other
as they stare hungrily
at the golf courses
while nearby the villas
draw back

CAROUSEL MAN

John T. Hendricks

Author's Reception: Pickett County, 1985

Do not disturb my hungry stars
As they devour my eyes
And give me joy in blindness—
For I become North Star
And heavens turn around my cup
Making me an absolute,
For I have no desire to stare at you
But have you stare at me.

TRAIL BLAZE

Albert R. Horrell

Across the valley night shades fall,
  And autumn mists drift down
To clothe the trees and hillside paths
  With mystic silver gown.

High on the hillside campfires glow
  Like stars with flickering light;
And down the trail the campers march
  Like fireflies in the night.

Below, the council fire flares,
  As campers gather near
To laugh and sing—and listen well
  Inspiring words to hear.

At evening's end the Scouts will climb
  Back to their dark camp sites;
And through the years they'll all recall
  Those happy outdoor nights.

AT THE AUDUBON SOCIETY

Alice Butler Howard

I've never seen a spoonbill
I'm sure I do not know
that it would add one cubit
to my present status quo.
But in order to astonish
and confound my haughty foe
I'd like to see a spoonbill
and firmly tell her so.

PARIS—1946

Marthalou Hunter

The Louvre had opened up again
and I was there on leave.
As I approached that grand old place
three soldiers, looking lost,
saluted me and asked,
  "Ma'am, what is that big old building there?"

I told them in a sentence
what it was, and added,
  "You'll see lots of things
  that you have seen before
  in school-books you have read."

They came with me
and gazed in silent awe
at everything we saw:
Venus de Milo, The Winged Victory,
even Mona Lisa back from hiding—
masterpieces by the score.

But no one spoke a word
until they stopped
before a painting hanging there
of peasants 'round the supper table.
The tall, slim mountain boy spoke out,
  "Oh, gosh, that looks like home."

AERIAL VIEW

Lore Jackson

A lone sojourner
Laboriously makes her way
Across a fierce desert.
I watch her approach
From the height
Of a peaked crag.
Her gait is familiar to me
As she struggles under
An awkward burden.
She continues slowly,
Often falling
To her knees.
She rises unsteadily
To her feet
Time and time again.
As she draws closer
The sense of the familiar
Grows more intense.
As she passes my crag
She turns her face up
To look at me.
I feel a sense of awe
And a sense of kinship
As I realize
That the green eyes
So deeply looking at me
Are my own.

ABOVE THE WORLD
(At the VanBuskirk's Mountain Home 1/1/87)

Ethelene Dyer Jones

Here on the mountain
 the Blue Ridges stretch
  like azure steeples
   from cathedrals of earth
    to the overarching sky.

Each crest lifts peaks
 in soundless praise
  to the Creator
   Architect of time and space.

His majesty and power
 beyond human description
  are written line upon line
   in the crenelated hills.

At times a veil of fog
 covers the valley below
  blocking civilization from view
   bringing quiet isolation.

Here we are above the world
 like eagles in an aerie
  sequestered in this stillness
   wrapped in a sentient vapor.

Here on the mountain
 above the cares and clamor
  tentacles circle to claim us
   but the call to valleys is stronger
    and this peace is relinquished to duty.

MY WORLD WAS TOO SMALL

Grover D. Jones

My world was too small;
It was what I could see;
I still was not tall
As soon I would be.

My world was too small,
Wanting all things I could see;
But I had never seen all,
Not even the sea.

I grew up to be tall;
A world waited for me.
Then came the strong call,
To go forth to see.

The blue mountains so tall
Hid the distance from me.
I must have a great call
If the world I would see.

So I heeded the call
And the strength came to me;
But I saw not quite all
Of the land and the sea.

My world has grown tall,
So broad and so high;
Now my world is all
So much larger than I.

WREN AND SONG

Susan A. Katz

The wrens returned again this spring
to nest within the wooden winter feeder
swinging from the maple's limb; impossibly
minute, the opening serves them now
for seasons beyond memory; smaller
than some snowflakes I have seen, they
stand their ground against all threats:
sparrow, blackbird, prowling tabby cat
and wake us every morning to the music
of their song; a sort of anguished challenge
hurled at dawn that reaffirms their lives;
confirming that against all odds
they still survive.

I think of them as our wrens, the same
as last year coming home again, and yet
the likelihood is generations of them
lived and died; perhaps, no lineage at all connects
them year to year, just some coincidental
happening attracts a mating pair to our yard and to
our feeder, convenient to their need;
and I suspect that we are not unlike them
in our journey through the centuries; we come
and go and pass this way or that and hurl, from
time to time the fact that we are here at all at
some deaf dawn; but in the grander plan
mattering not one bit less than wren and song;
not one bit more than here and gone.

MOMENT OF SLEEP

Harriet Stovall Kelley

Sleep—
    the moment when all thoughts,
     returning
    to narrow towers of the mind,
     beat their wings
    and flutter, failing; wearily
     fold pale feathers
    and settle in the shadows of
     still chimes.

Yet
    even in the drifting dark
     their softly
    restless whispering of breath
     can still
    be told—a quivering as in
     the hull
    of a bell, long after the note
     is pealed.

Dim
    through the dusk of dreams
      they still are seen:
        a moonwhite curve . . .
          the shape of a wing . . .
            a dovegrey murmuring . . .

CENTERING

Patricia Kirby

Stare into the center of the sun
and wonder at its leaping
wildly side to side as though
tempted to depart its boundaries —
or reveling in its limits circumscribed.

Unlike Lucifer the earth
in its brief shining morning hour
toying with the idea of rebellion
against all natural order
of creation — pauses
at the edge of anarchy, before
daring to war with stars
that, too, may fade and fall.

Will it center itself in time?
Like art? To a measured rhyme?

Stare at the center of the sun
and it dances, as at Fatima!
As the prophet leapt for joy
when the circle was complete.

THE LAST TIME MY GRANDFATHER HELD MY HAND

Nancy Treu Klotz

The last time my grandfather held my hand
the northern wind crafted a lusty charge
against the window pane.
I heard its swooping cry
and crossed the threshold to my grandfather's bed
which was placed against the wall
as long as I could remember.
His strength had waned and his voice sighed.
The times and friends of old must have
filled the sleepy corners of his thoughts
about long forgotten places.
There was no moment of farewell,
only of tomorrow and the slumber through the
looms of night interlacing its gentle deliverance.
It was this moment I never forgot—his one last
reach for the child,
In a touch which grasps the fingers from old to young
where feeling flows in peaceful splendor.

OLD FRIENDS ARE LIKE OLD WINE

John Ransom Lewis

Old friends are like old wine;
They suit the taste—
Like wine, the choicest years
Leave none to waste.

Old friendship may be chilled,
Though never so cold
But they warm the distance and years
Like wine of old.

Labels can't depict
What lies inside,
For friends hold more than labels
Can ever hide.

So I savor vintage friends
And vintage wine—
No promise of vintners says
How long they're mine!

GONE FISHING

M. Rosser Lunsford

When my time comes for the rocking chair
I won't be rocking and wishing,
Instead you'll find that I'm not there
But that I've gone a-fishing.

When my time comes for bedroom slippers
Look under my bed for mine,
For I'll be wearing skippers
And using my hook and line.

When my time comes for the 'satin-box'
There'll be no chance to rescind,
And I'll have no tackle box
Nor fishing friends and kin.

When my time comes for His Pearly Gate
And if I should be missing,
You will know He let me wait
So I could go a-fishing.

RITUAL

Peggy Zuleika Lynch

Squaring relations with Great Spirit
bowing traditionally to East and West
South and North, piping my peace,
smoke cobwebbing brain's fissures,
I dance my dance to drum beats
not so heavy, not so steady
in a one woman pow-wow.

FRIENDSHIP

Kay Magenheimer

My balloon skims the air as easily
And notedly as, without moving a limb,
A swimmer with flair floats on water.

All the world looks up to see
My hard-run balloon shining in the sky—
Obliged as the moon to an absentee sun.

No stop, I thought, to its flight when suddenly,
Without warning, it lands atop a tree. Pops! Bursts!
Even before noon, and within sight of the loons

Who notice not, in the end,
That ever important string
Safely ringed in the hand of a friend.

AND *YOU* WISH TO SPEAK TO *ME*

Betty Maine

As I stood at the sink
washing dishes,
all immersed in suds,
I glanced out the window
to three children at play.
They knelt in a circle,
all immersed in a game,
while a little dog
sat, watching,
all immersed in them.
Washing, playing, watching;
engrossed in our world,
yet a part of each other.
The dog broke the spell
by moving out of place.
Being of simple mind
and following his heart,
he sat upon their game
and got them to look up.

I REMEMBER

Frank McKemie

On a cold but sunny morning
trees stand in winter's bareness
on grassy shores of the lake.
Though planes roar overhead,
Nature seems at peace here.
It is a boon to sit in silence
and renew one's soul.

How we are driven daily
like fallen leaves before an angry wind!
The sights and sounds of scenes
too often erotic, erratic, or absurd
crowd in upon our anxious senses.
The drum, drum, drum
of a shrill world hawking its wares
may drown the inner voice
that carries our saving messages.

I sit by the quiet lapping waters
and see again the keen eyes and busy fingers
of one who guided me through early years,
her faith that she lived in a purposeful world
and I would share that faith—
a strong voice calling me to renewal.

CICADA'S SONG

Beth Ragan Minski

Five years dormant underground,
fetally sucking sweet tree sap,
the cicada nymph cracks its skin,
to emerge mature on the resilient trunk.

Like the hum of high tension wires,
he drums his ear-piercing cry
to court a silent green wife.

Directed by his sibilant song,
she sails to his trunk
to rendezvous and mate.

For five weeks he drones the constant chorus,
while she ravishes the forest burrowing eggs,
unless waylaid by a praying mantis
or ambushed by a blue jay's beak.

TIME IS FLEETING

Albert E. Mitchell

Time is fleeting, I am older
Sometimes bolder, sometimes bleating
Youth is passing, age is here
Wisdom is near, yet vacillating.
Are we learning of heaven so far
or just bleating till time ends here?
Give time a beating—learn what's near,
For isn't the clearing about the afar
Or are we despairing away the hours?
Hours are endearing, minutes are dear.
Seconds are pressing our end nearer
Nothing knowing till we lie in our bier.

WHAT MATTERS

Mikki Griffis Morris

It matters not the color of one's face
Much love abounds for the whole human race.
It matters not the language that we speak
The language of the soul is what we seek.
It matters not the feel of people's skin
Life's vital force glows brightly from within.
And matters less the oddities of mind
When good and beauty dwell in all we find.

It matters not the age   the sex   or creed
It's God in others we will always need.

SITUATION REPORT

John K. Ottley, Jr.

We have, love, settled into our respective firebases.
We send out patrols to probe
the wire and minefields surrounding
each other's positions.
Inevitably they return reporting no contact
with the enemy.
We recon by fire
lobbing a few mortar rounds
into each other's redoubts, but
that fails to provoke a decisive engagement,
only counter battery fire.
Occasionally, our forward listening posts
exchange good-natured catcalls
before they resume sniping.
Daily our engineer units inspect our defensive perimeters
shoring up any gap in the lines
where intimacy might infiltrate.
Our real feelings about each other
are safe from incoming artillery
deep in sandbagged bunkers
hidden from aerial observation by camouflage nets.
We issue hopeful communiques
to our allies: "Everything's fine at the front;
we have plenty of chow and ammo."
We have sacrificed freedom of maneuver.
We no longer have a strategy for victory
but calmly wait to see
who will retreat first.
As of 0600 today, sir,
I scanned the area to our front
and there were no messengers
bearing white flags.

ED

Marie W. Ovrevik

The Lord's love overflowed the day
That Ed was born,
And so a little extra bit
Was given him to keep.
But he, in turn, would share this love
With everyone he met.
His eyes showed love—his voice spoke love,
And we who knew him
Will not soon forget.
Though he is gone,
Wherever he may be
I know he spreads his love around
The way he did to me.

PIECES OF MOUNTAINS

June Owens

he gave small creekbed
stones to her
said he would drill
them for beads
loop her neck
with pieces of mountains and he
kept his word

they are not so
heavy as she had
imagined   full
of amorous brightness
that rain makes brighter
and to which winter
gives different voices
when they tap
together   higher
pitched than in
summer when the beads
lie warm and lazy
over her breasts
warm and lazy
as his hands

THE AMSTERDAM DANCER

B. Ashley Parker, Sr.

Be calm, my heart
    and other appendages
        'tis merely lust
    that stirs you so
Think not of her
    as one so fair
        for her harlot ways
    lewdly show.

Her limbs they sway
    like seductive palms
        beckoning those who
    gaze anew
Like innocent lads
    to a fairyland drawn
        her charms will
    draw you, too.

Her lips are soft
    like summer rain
        her nectar
    sweet to taste
But in a web
    of the widow's clutch
        will be he
    who succumbs in haste.

Just view her there
    as one might view
        a sculpture
    made of stone
For there is no heart
    in the maiden beast
        only poison
    in her bones.

BETH

Evelyn Hoge Pendley

There she sits astride her mare,
Straight and smiling, in control.
Her dog and cat play by the fence,
And nearby is a frisky foal.

Her flowers dot spots in the yard
Where birds swoop down for baths and grain,
Where grassy fields and great green trees
Thrive in bright sunshine or warm rain.

Within, mementos fill small nooks.
Her artwork captivates much space.
Off in a corner, her guitar
Suggests soft music and sweet grace.

Her scrapbooks hold brief records of
Some cherished moments of her past,
Of fleeting youth, of friendships formed,
Of dreams that came and did not last.

There have been times she's scrounged around
For paper and a stamp or so
To send a message and enclose
Some clever camera shots that show

Subjects she loves. Her words reveal
Her insights for perceptive art,
Her faith in God, her caring soul,
The longings of her secret heart.

FASCINATION FOR EDGES

Pat Morton Posey

There is rapture in the half-light of the moon
  dissolving into shadows of the hedges
  the kitten feels excitement in the hour,
  beckoned by the silent urge of edges.

There is rapture in the half-light of the moon
  when chills of evening slide by garden posts
  and porch lights circle scarlet primrose blooms
  that whiten into tiny gathering ghosts.

There is rapture in the half-light of the moon
  when blazing sun-clouds fan into twilight
  and obdurate twitters of a whippoorwill
  balance on sharp edges of the night.

There is rapture in the half-light of the night.

GRANDMOTHER

Kay Kempton Raade

When newness filled her walk
and buttercups more than
snow-covered dreams, she was
long and thin as the lodge-
pole pines she swung high
to make the framework
of her days. Weight of years
and pull from Mother Earth
has bowed the black-wrapped
legs. Her shape peared
as shoulders gave their square
to slope. The tracks through
her leathered face aim toward
the ground.
        But around the eyes
burst the rays of the Sun
                in all directions
when she smiles.
The tears that lay in basined
lids reflect
two worlds.

KRISTINA

Zhanna P. Radar

An old sweater —
you let me have it
before moving far away.
Soft and light,
the wool brushing against my skin,
it holds warm memories.

And your clogs — remember?
New, but too bulky for your luggage . . .
They stand on duty by the door,
outside slippers,
waiting for my children and me —
especially when the yard
is drenched with rain or dew,
or when snow
softens red Georgia clay.

Though well-worn now,
they still clomp merrily
on the sidewalk; and in the grass
they seem to whisper
Kristina-Kristina-Kristina . . .

THE FISH HATCHERY NIGHT CHOIR

Jack A. Ransbottom

Oh, that nighttime thunder of the male bullfrogs,
The "jug-o-rum" chorus at night, all bass so deep,
Where we waded the shallows with a miner's lamp
Shined into grass on the levees where they creep.

Each an omnivorous feeder with folded tongue
That lashes out to pull in any moving prey.
The big man said, "Kill them and their eggs."
His crop goldfish; he thought frogs cut his pay.

We waded out to dip buckets under their egg rafts,
Threw them on the levees where they once did sing,
Shot the croakers and caused a silent funeral,
Then mourned the chorus night would never bring.

STARTING THE DAY

Evelyn S. Rineer

It is good to wake up in the morning
And throw the covers down,
And say to myself, with firm resolve,
"I'll push the world around".

Some say it is automatic,
That one with sense can see
A man does not push a button,
The earth's movement is free.

Inside me, I know better;
Before ever my feet "touch ground",
I have to say to myself each day:
"I must push this old world around".

Somehow the day is happy,
I rise with a smile, not a frown,
When I sing my own private theme song:
"I must push this old world around".

I pretend he is out there waiting,
Still, without any sound—and
It is up to me for him to be free,
When I rise and push him around.

So maybe I do shut one eye, or two—
To those serious ones who frown,
But I know that I show more joy as I go,
When I push this old world around.

LINES FOR A WEDDING
NEAR MOUNTAINTOWN CREEK
for Julia and Bill

Bettie Sellers

Kneeling by the creekbank,
a potter scoops red Georgia clay,
molds sweeping walls, vital forms—
as you have shaped my life
taller, straighter,
stronger with renewed purpose.

With brush and colors
sifted from the soft earth,
the master draws faces, flowers
on waiting clay walls,
as you have marked bold new designs
on my every waking day,
fresh patterns on my nightly dreams.

Then this vessel
is placed within the fire's heat.
Darker colors begin to glow,
shimmer into pure reds and blues,
and love has lighted my whole being
into dancing flames of delight,
bright embers of peace and joy.

Today, my love,
as we stand here together,
hand clasped in hand beside the creek,
each has been potter,
each in turn the clay.
Together we have molded days,
fired moments
until this present dear time,
when the potters and the clays
have become as one.

WITH THE WILD BEASTS*

Jeanne Osborne Shaw

Did the lion come roaring past the rocks
As if it were hungering for His hunger,
And did He fear those bristling locks,
Thinking that Satan might have Him at last?
Then did He remember the lion was no stronger
Than Daniel's angel could hold fast?

Did the wild goat peer from a thorny throne,
And He wish that freedom to be His own,
But remember that Moses drove it thundering
To the woods where Israel's sin was hurled?
Did He speak to it kindly, loving and wondering
If His back were strong for sins of the world?

When the eagle dived from a molten sky,
Did He cover His face and, sorrowing, ponder
If escaping Hades meant losing an eye?
Then did angels fill Him with wonder
That He should mount up on eagles' wings
Above all screaming earthly things?

Did the fox, brown stopper in his hole,
Look craftily toward His rumpled robe?
As He wanted bread to share with that cunning,
Did He reflect that lands could unroll
As His to command and His to probe,
But no home offered a pallet from running?

Did He see a snake with fetters of staring
Bind fast a dove in a motionless Hell
And dread that Satan would burn the wood
Of a tree that held His cross in its bearing?
Then did He recall the dove over the Flood
And know He had power over Lucifer's spell?

*Mark 1:13

187

UNLEAVENED POET

Polly Shaw

I'll tell you why I can't make poems
Blend those strange ingredients with them:
Because when I pour heart into words
It causes curdles in the rhythm

And when I measure the beat-beat-beat
That makes perfection in time
Words gloop-glop all over locutions
And I forget they're supposed to rhyme

And theme! Ah, theme   how that eludes me
That tantalizing vagary
I sift its wisdom   taste its folly
From Dear Abby to Du Barry

Still its virtue eschews my vision
And with capricious whimsy
Crumbles my lofty-leavened crotchets
Into trivia so flimsy

That not a single soul can see
A Browning in my noggin
But all is not lost, my dear Odgen
My Wallbanger cake'll frost your nogden!

GREAT-GRANDMOTHER'S PORTRAIT

Maurine Smith

In Mississippi, after the Civil War, Grandfather
Loaded his family into a covered wagon
Wrapped your portrait in a faded quilt
Moved to Texas to begin a new life
Built a house on the banks of the Brazos River
Hung your portrait in its parlor and
Taught his children grace and gentility.

Orphaned at nineteen, my father
Sold his horse and saddle
Kissed his mother good-by
Sewed your portrait in a sheet
Caught a train to Indian Territory
Fell in love with Cricket and married her
Built her a home and hung your portrait
Beside one of her Cherokee grandmother.

Helped Cricket rear their children. When he
Died during the depression, I
Claimed your portrait as my birthright
Packed my family into my old sedan
Drove them to Santa Fe, New Mexico
Built them an adobe house
Hung your portrait on its central wall
Watched my children grow under your eyes.

Plagued with age and infirmities, before I
Gave you to my son to treasure for his son, I
Pictured you when you posed for the artist.
You wore your widow's weeds and old lady's cap
Honored your late husband, a steamboat captain,
Tucked his tintype in the broach at your throat
Framed it with a circle of your braided hair
Arranged your weeds in discreet folds
Leaned back in your rose colored chair, and
Sat for the artist who brought you to life
For the descendants you never knew.

A CASUAL ACQUAINTANCE RECALLED
(For Loren Eiseley)

Bruce Souders

A half a century later,
I still remember him well:
face scarred by care,
the weather-wizened face
of a dirt farmer; eyes
emitting eagerness for company,
not loneliness and sorrow
as I expected from one
so battered by events and time.

The Great Depression had not
destroyed his will to live.
The tales that he told as we sat
by the fire, drinking a brew
from old vegetable cans, aroused
my desire to take to the rails,
extending the drive to devour
adventure I had found in books
when I took from my friend the prize
for reading in school that year.

I had no fear of him,
this new-found idol of mine
whom family and friends dismissed
with a snarl: "He's just a hobo."

At this point in time I wonder:
"Was he the refugee
from insecurity
whose strange hours on rails
were but an interlude
in his immense journey
into anthropology?"

SOME PEOPLE NEVER LEARN

Thomas Paul Spahos

Life's a powerful teacher
But some people never learn
To give instead of taking
To share instead of breaking

Life's a powerful teacher
But some people never learn
To be strong, gentle and kind
To admire all humankind

Life's a powerful teacher
But some people never learn
To love children and spouses
To honor all God's Houses

Life's a powerful teacher
But some people never learn
To trust sweet nature and bees
To protect fresh streams and trees

Life's a powerful teacher
But some people never learn
Till their friends have moved and gone
Till they're old and all alone

IN SHADOW'S WAKE

Leland Staven

A superblot, horizon centered,
This steel island's rock-ripped hull
Pours out a smothering petro-cloud.
It blankets the water's crystalline face,
A dark shroud for this dying place.

Oily black and irridescent,
The moving liquid-shadow's wake
Eclipses the pristine pebbled beach,
Now quite beyond nature's reach.

Thick viscoid tongues of tar
Lap up and then cover-consume
The slow moving forms of life.
Now all are beyond survival's strife.

Wrapped and trapped in crude-oil coats,
Fish, birds and animals
Slowly expire in terror's grip,
A nightmare from the super ship.

A spreading shiny obsidian sea
Reflects a growing techno-greed.
This Rorschach blot as seen from space,
A warning sign, the fate of our place.

DOWN A COUNTRY LANE

Rebekah Stion

Strolling down a country lane
Where memories are made

Winding a path cut through the woods
Of a beautiful shade

Listening to the tune of the wind
Blowing through the branches

Walking this path through the brush
Taking my chances

Seeing the animals scattered about
Their beauty in color arrayed

Feeling complete freedom
As nature all around me displayed

Enjoying this peace
Letting my mind grasp this life

Knowing at times
It seems filled with much strife

Calling high above me
A bird responds to its mate

Stopping I notice how
Sweet the music they make

Appreciating this and my adventure
I turn back toward home

Leaving a part of myself
On this country lane I often roam.

"Take time to enjoy the beauty of God's creation. You'll
find freedom and a peace there that we sometime forget."

"FAST FORWARD"

Eileen Stratidakis

I no longer remember
all the places I have lived;
there have been too many moves.
Neighborhoods look the same
though twenty years have passed.

You ask whether the wrinkles
in your neck make you look old,
if I think you could still attract
a girl of twenty-nine.
I recall younger Sundays

When all that mattered was writing,
being together like this
with other poets.
The year is getting colder;
we never made it to the beach.

Overhead long lines
of birds are making their way
to Florida. If only
our own maps could be
so clearly drawn.

NO INDIANS COME OVER THE HILL

Paula L. Stricklin

A bird is all I see up on the knoll;
He hops and pecks to find a bug or worm,
His head and tail abob against the blue
And clouds that float above the rise like huge
Balloons attached to frills of summer muse,
But no Indian rides over the hill
   On galloping cayuse.

At dusk I wait below the rise; perhaps
This time the wind is right and signs of stars
And call of fowl. The eyes of night begin
To stare at me—reflecting Gemini
A cat is stalking prey and poised to strike—
But no Indians loom over the hill
   With faces painted stripes.

The oak that guards the sleeping vale is bare;
Her branches hold the rounded moon as though
It were the final fruit of autumn's store;
The naked arms of other trees extend
Above the rise to seize the silvered gourd,
But no Indians scream over the hill
   With frosted whoops of war.

THE HEIRLOOM

Denver Stull

Please do not sit in this old chair,
For it's my place, you see;
It's where I sit when I can spare
Some time for reverie.

You see there where the seat sinks in?
I think a spring is broke.
Right here the fabric's wearing thin;
The frame is good white oak.

But this old chair just suits me fine;
It seems that when I sit
Our contours seem to run in line,
Because I slump a bit.

I know it does not look too nice
Here in the living room,
But I just cannot sacrifice
This priceless old heirloom

DYING BREATH

Jimmy Terrell

The late August breeze
tunes the grass harp
and creates a shiver
on the diseased red oak.
A headless grave
in the red Georgia clay
Lies at peace, within and without.
The kinfolk, friends and well-wishers
are long gone, save the last
strains of the song,
"Shall We Gather at the River?"
Memories of another day,
another time, another place,
have taken flight
and now dance
with the mulberry leaves
on the dying breath of August.

A POET'S LAMENT

Katharine Theiling

What can I say
that hasn't been said
about flowers and trees,
the buzz of bees,
the blue of the sky,
clouds floating by;
the warmth of the sun
and, when day is done,
stars twinkling bright,
the moon sending light
on the earth below.

What can I say
that hasn't been said
about birds and their song
singing all the day long;
about the heart and soul,
about love or a goal,
the tears of a child
or the charm of a smile?
Of the poems I've read,
everything's been said;
so why try to write any more?

NEBRASKA

Charles R. Tucker

A State of contrast.
  The State of adventure.
A State of dreams come true.
  The State of panoramic view.

  N-e-b-r-a-s-k-a's
. . . . just waiting for you!

Let Nebraska . . . Attract 'ya!

A lot of nostalgia.
  The pioneering spirit.
A blend of rich history.
  The life of folk lore.

  N-e-b-r-a-s-k-a's
. . . . just waiting for you!

Let Nebraska . . . Attract 'ya!

A State of country music jamborees.
  The State of 'special' memories.
A State of arts and crafts shows.
  The State that, "Heaven knows?"

  N-e-b-r-a-s-k-a's
. . . . just waiting for you!

Let Nebraska . . . Attract 'ya!

BONSAI

Memye Curtis Tucker

What tree wouldn't
like to live forever—
misted,
pruned, wired,
breathed over
until
it's
a fierce shape
against wind, the
crash
of
ocean,
the heavy downward pull of time?

COVENTRY CATHEDRAL

Tommie Wells Ulrich

Shattered shell of former glory
Stark reminder of bombing
Ghostly skeleton carefully tended
Symbol of man's abiding faith.

From debris of war's devastation
Melded from nails of ancient edifice
The cross stands above rugged altar
Formed of stones from crumbling walls.

Crafted of stone of latter days
Forever linked to timeworn walls
Soaring aloft like Phoenix rising
A new cathedral stands.

Ineffable sweetness of choirboys' voices
Surrounding radiance of golden light
Stabs the heart in breathless wonder
And fills the soul with awe.

"J. J."

Emily Blake Vail

J. J. sits in the sun, shining.

Even when days are dreary
and the rain snakes down
slanted plate glass windows,
J. J. shines, his movements
rhythmical as a fiddle player's.

The shoes stand upright
soon to be made shiny, like new.
They recognize a maestro.

Keep on shining, J. J., I say.
He can never quite remember my name,
but I know all about his kids.
He has a daughter in California,
doing well in college. His son lives
with his "ahnt" in Tennessee, plays
basketball. Studying, too, he hopes.

Never unhappy, never down.
The steady of the shoeshine stand.

One day he came dressed up in a suit.
I been at the City Council, he says.
I been told 'em all about the slum lords,
about the rats big as cats, about all
the broken locks and the needy children,
about the toilets not ever working.
When I finish, they stand up for me
and cheer, ten minutes they clapped,
Miss . . . He didn't remember my name.

J. J., you're a hero, a great person, I
say. I should tell kids everywhere about you.
Tell 'em about working, he instructs me.
Hard work means they'll have long life,
and they'll always feel good and happy.

So J. J. has to be a poem.

TABLEAU

Virginia Cole Veal

Through windows of
transparent glass
the late winter sun

flits over brass—and old lace
spills across silver candlesticks
collects in reflections
on the polished
oak table
and on me
I pour your tea . . .
                    and wait.

UNASSUMING KNIGHT

Golda Foster Walker

At times almost inaudibly, you speak:
your voice, though soft, conveys a knightliness,
inspiring me to feel more queen than wife,
enhancing all the facets of my life.
You have no errant eye—and I would seek
no replica of you—a man unique,
whose depth of loyalty is fathomless,
whose chivalry and love sustain and bless.
Nobility does not demand a crown,
nor rituals. This truth is handed down
through time, for worthy noblemen are born
when they accept the flower *and* the thorn.
And muteness could not mar your eloquence
nor minimize your stature as a prince.

ATLAS THE FAITHFUL

Betty Abernathy Wallace

Could one blame Atlas? He wished to abdicate
his heavy role, perhaps shift it to Hercules.
And not entirely because the physical weight
wore him down, nor that the majestic trees,
mountain points or jagged rocks made the task
so intolerable that his massive shoulders
sagged beneath the load. He could mask
discomfort easily, bearing up under the boulders
light heartedly — if the world respected him.

He thought sometimes that Zeus and all other
godheads deliberately snubbed, neglected him.
Still, he cradled the sphere gentle as a mother.
Within giant strength, Atlas hoped against hope
that he gave mankind time to grow in scope.

SHAKESPEARE FESTIVAL REMEMBERED: YALE, 1960

James E. Warren, Jr.

School once was swirling leaves
out of the oak and the maple;
and I saw the world grow dapple
with autumn and geography
and with that gently intellectual sea
which lyrically laves
the shore of childhood with a teasing tide
of maps and music down October's red.

Now thirty years more dazzling,
our books are opened at
the slow lips and the throat
of verse. Professors thunderously muse
at drops of beauty drizzling
on kings and battles and significant swords
and on men's hopes too terrible to lose—
more giant and more wonderful their words!

And through the window winds would caress
a leaf and a leaf that whispered, "Guess!"

FANTASY

Connie Smith Watson

I stood silent, while the plumes of yearning soared
Like tiny pastel birds,
Rising and painting a rainbow
Of the possible,
Until I realized that I must cage them,
Clip their wings, and grieve
That they would never soar again.

EXTRAPOLATION

Gus Wentz

The view up rocky road
Soared into azure acres overhead
Whose billowy blotches,
Superimposed in such a style
As hints of subtle high sky art,
Allowed the blue to simmer through.
The pebbled path, itself, runs rutted
Betwixt two trailer rows
(Euphemistically, "mobile homes",
though their lone travel is apt to be downward,
by decay or fire, to ash to ground)—
Sparse shelter for these inaffluents
To call home,
But better than a sidewalk sleep.
And yet, they ride and read and revel
In far greater comfort—
Thanks to taunt technology—
Than Louis XIV, Henry VIII
Or even Harry Truman ever knew.

FAITH

Joy B. Wix

The sky was dark and we could hardly see
I ran outside and brought the kittens in
they drank warm milk and cuddled close to me
we slept in peace beside the fireplace bin.

Winds howled and streaks of sleet fell through the night
as on an artist' palette; they had spread
small Domino and Golden Red as light
bright colors danced around each furry head.

Next morning yellow canvas stretched the floor
the Artist brush found us entwined and warm
His hand embellished us with hope and lore
then dreams came true without too much alarm.

Our faith restores the marvel found in life
Leads us to march on to new drums and fife.

LOVE IS LETTING GO

Harriet Fay Woodcock

I would possess ye heart and soul
Because I love ye so.
But if loving is to be my goal,
Then I must let ye go.

For ye are one of nature's free,
Who must fly your own course,
And not be trapped by the likes of me,
To live life with remorse.

I see thee smiling through my tears,
For ye are not all mine.
Yet I could not have last the years,
Had I not been part thine.

AMANDA IN STATE

Dorothy Williamson Worth

There she lies
amid rose-colored satin and pale lace
white hair perfectly styled
that familiar half-smile frozen
on her lips
beautiful even in death.

The town comes in a steady stream
pausing beside her to murmur
in hushed tones how natural she looks
careful to sign the Guest Register.

We stand in a line, pressing hands
receiving words of comfort
an occasional hug or kiss
from those we call friends . . .
and the tears will not come.

I am next to her
and I wait
for her to speak
in well-bred accent
to tell me how to stand
what to say to Great Aunt Sarah
or to mention reluctantly
that my dress
is hardly suitable
for this occasion.

But she is silent at last
and I join the others
in yet another performance
of lifelong duty to the family
and to her.

De mortuis nil nisi bonum.

And God have mercy
on the survivors.

CHURCHYARD
(Trinity Churchyard, Stratford-Upon-Avon)

E. Jerome Zeller

No sound of
Avon's
Steady
Flow
> Disturbs the
> Stones
> Well-
> Anchored
> Here.
Hushed
Prayers
Hover
In the
Shade;
> Sparse
> Thanksgivings
> Rise
> Upon
Infrequent
Sunlight
Shafts. The
> Dead
> Sigh
> Silence,
> Slipping
Through
Thoughtless
Time
Like the
> River
> Flows,
> Without
> Memory's
> Meaning;
Lost in
Shadow'd
Peace.

212

EVEN THE AZALEAS ARE BEGINNING TO DROOP

Patricia Zeller

Eyes still closed, she slowly strokes the
  muslin sheet with fingers dry and gnarled
While droning swirl of ceiling fan marks
  night's demise and dawn's appearance.
Poised between two worlds, she'll decide
  again which one it shall be.
No earthly reason for her to be here, they often say.
And yet, so far, she's refused to fold
  her tents and fade away.
This week, for the first time, she has
  seriously thought of doing just that.
Maybe it's the lack of rain. Can't
  go on much longer, they say.
Drying everything up. Slowly squeezing out
  the green, making way for brown and grey,
Affects a person, after all,
  her body, spirit, head.
Behind closed eyes play myriad images
  of moisture-starved trees whose
Usual verdant dance has slowed to
  panting crawl. Beyond her walls
Even the azaleas are beginning to droop.
  What's it all for? Time to decide.
Better to break clean than to yield to
  slow desiccation by an arid atmosphere.
Thirstily, what is beyond her
  sucks each drop of water, blood, marrow
Till her parched, brittle frame mirrors
  the remnant garden where
Even the azaleas are beginning to droop.

Soft droplets of cosmic rain released
  by some giant, celestial sponge
Might stop in time her fading—and the garden's.
But she will choose this dawn, behind
  closed eyes, and she will go away.
No earthly reason for her to be here now that
  even the azaleas are beginning to droop.

SOCIETY PAGES

GEORGIA STATE POETRY SOCIETY, INC.

Founded August 30, 1979
Incorporated June 11, 1981
Atlanta, Georgia

Member, NATIONAL FEDERATION OF STATE POETRY
SOCIETIES, INC.
Affiliate, ACADEMY OF AMERICAN POETS

Eleventh Year
July 1, 1989–June 30, 1990

OFFICERS AND COMMITTEE CHAIRS

President, Dr. Frank McKemie
Vice President, Dr. Edward DeZurko
Treasurers, Harry Shaw and John Ottley, Jr.
Secretary, Neil Fraser
Publicity, Charles Dickson
Finance, Jo Ann Yeager Adkins
Membership, Virginia Dickson
Members' Readings, Herbert Denmark
Book Reviews, Virginia Veal
Newsletter, Ethelene Dyer Jones
Newsletter Contest Chair, Julia Evatt
Librarian, Dr. E. Jerome Zeller
Mailings, Riherd Greene
       Edna Greene
Stophes Reporter, Jeanne Osborne Shaw
The Reach of Song Editor, Jo Ann Yeager Adkins
Quarterly Contests, Marthalou Hunter
Youth Contests, Rebekah Stion
Byron Herbert Reece Contest, Virginia Veal

MEMBERSHIP 1989–1990

Melanie Rawls Abrams, Atlanta
Jo Ann Yeager Adkins, Atlanta
Carole G. Anderson, Acworth
Aurelia Austin, Atlanta
Trudy K. Austin, Hartwell
Kenneth W. Baker, Atlanta
Heather Ballew, College Park
Frances Lee Barber, Fairburn
Mildred Barthel, Mr. Vernon, Iowa
Walter J. Bartling, Decatur
James Andy Batemen, Hazelhurst, Mississippi
William J. Beshears, Winder
Richard G. Beyer, Florence, Alabama
Jeffrey H. Biggers, Dunwoody
Lethe Hunter Bishop, Atlanta
Ronald Lathem Boring, Douglasville
Ruth M. Bowen, Atlanta
Melissa Bower, Augusta
Dorothy Brooks, Atlanta
Diana E. Brown, Atlanta
Marel Brown, Decatur
Renee Brown, Atlanta
Tina Brown, Woodstock
Charles J. Bruehler, Atlanta
Lexton Buchanan, Smyrna
Imogene McAfee Buder, Decatur
Archie P. Buie, Cleveland
Angela Burns, St. Simons Island
Ernest Camp, Jr., Monroe
Patricia E. Canterbury, Sacramento, California
Margery V. Carlson, Snellville
Helen H. Carnes, Atlanta
Wil Carter, East Point
Sarah M. Carver, Tucker
Mary Chase, Atlanta
Mary F. Childs, Royston
Maggie H. Cohn, Austell
Mary Ann Coleman, Athens
Mary Catherine Comisky, Smyrna
Jerome A. Connor, Atlanta
Della Martin Cook, Forest Park
Mary Nell Corley, Winter Haven, Florida
Charles E. Cravey, Warner Robins
Diane Ramsey Criss, Winder
Geraldine Crocker, Atlanta
William L. Davenport, Big Canoe
Carita D. Dawson-Ford, St. Simons Island
Peter Dean, Decatur
Beverly Denmark, Decatur
Delores Denmark, Decatur

Herbert Walter Denmark, Decatur
Edward R. DeZurko, Athens
Grace DeZurko, Athens
Charles B. Dickson, Doraville
Virginia P. Dickson, Doraville
Harriet Jo Dilbeck, Marietta
Mary Ann Doe, Alpharetta
Irma Dowis-Edwards, Stockbridge
Pat Dozier, Montezuma
Ellen Dugan, Atlanta
Nellie P. Duke, Carrollton
Bill Early, Griffin
Flora Eberhart, Alpharetta
Lota Vickers Elliott, APO New York
Jane Porter Ennis, Decatur
Nelle Branan Ennis, Albany
Jewel Rowland Evans, Stockbridge
Julia E. Evatt, Ellijay
Russell Farmer, Spartanburg
Carole B. Fessenden, Gainesville
Denise F. Forbes, Hampton
Beverly Anne Forsyth, Woodstock
Barbara Fraser, Atlanta
Neil L. Fraser, Atlanta
Stephen D. Fraser, Atlanta
Bernard I. Garland, Atlanta
Evelyn Garland, Atlanta
Al Garvin, Winder
Roberta George, Valdosta
Alyce Gondek, Stone Mountain
Betty Lou Gore, Decatur
Mildred Greear, East Point
Connie J. Green, Lenoir City, Tennessee
James L. Green, East Point
R. Michael Green, Decatur
Edna Greene, Doraville
R. Riherd Greene, Doraville
Bruce Greenfield, Doraville
William G. Griffin, Rome
Anthony Grooms, Atlanta
Janet Habas, Atlanta
Thelma R. Hall, Rome
Wilson Hall, Rome
Maxine Hamm, Doraville
Elizabeth Ann Hammill, Athens
Barbara Harris Harper, Gainesville
Mavis H. Harrell, Nashville
Leonard P. Harris, Reading, Pennsylvania
Lynn Farmer Harris, Decatur
Cowan M. Hart, Jr., Conyers
Jane L. Hart, Conyers
Susan G. Harvey, Rome

Scarlet Dawn Hay, Fort Valley
Margaret Hayes, Atlanta
Robert W. Hays, Marietta
Beverly V. Head, Atlanta
John T. Hendricks, Griffin
Anne E. Hendricks, Griffin
Georgia T. Henry, Atlanta
Rick T. Herren, Martinez
Alison Herren, Martinez
Dekie Hicks, Decatur
Albert R. Horrell, Harvester, Missouri
Alice Butler Howard, Atlanta
Ruby P. Humphries, Rome
Marthalou Hunter, Atlanta
Victoria Hunter, Decatur
Dorothy Enge Hutcheson, Temple
Akbar Imhotep, Atlanta
Lore Ann Jackson, Waco, Texas
William Jefcoat, Atlanta
Jane Johnson, Norcross
Marion Smith Johnson, Atlanta
Debbie Jones, Statham
Donna N. Jones, Statesboro
E. Keith Jones, Statham
Ethelene Dyer Jones, Epworth
Grover D. Jones, Epworth
Susan A. Katz, Monsey, New York
Harriet Stovall Kelley, Dallas, Texas
Patricia Kirby, Atlanta
Nancy Treu Klotz, Atlanta
Charles Carroll Lamb, Albany
Margaret R. Leggat, Riverdale
Ann E. Lewis, Atlanta
John Ransom Lewis, Jr., Atlanta
John Lieb, Decatur
Russel A. Ligeikis, Mountain Rest, South Carolina
Kathleen B. Lindsey, Atlanta
Sally Lockhart, Lakemont
Joan H. Loeb, Atlanta
Jeanne Losey, Shelbyville, Tennessee
Robert S. Lowrance, Atlanta
M. Rosser Lunsford, Douglasville
Peggy Zuleika Lynch, Austin, Texas
Betty Flood Lyon, Demorest
Kay Magenheimer, Carrollton
Betty Maine, Gainesville
Catharine P. Maze, St. Simons Island
Edith McCann, East Point
Robin McCants, Decatur
Judith A. McCourd, Atlanta
Betty B. McKemie, Avondale Estates
Frank McKemie, Avondale Estates

Frank M. McKenney, Macon
Jannelle Jones McRee, East Point
Lillian Newham McRee, Valdosta
Barbara A. McWilliams, Studio City, California
Beth Ragan Minski, Roswell
Albert E. Mitchell, Jekyll Island
Hazel Mitchell, Lilburn
Francie Mizell, Doraville
Janice Townley Moore, Young Harris
Mikki Griffis Morris, Brunswick
June Naiman, Lakeland, Florida
R. Grayson Newman, Ducktown, Tennessee
Mary Sue Norsworthy, Stockton
Jane S. Ogilvie, Atlanta
Marjorie G. Ohrtmann, Atlanta
John K. Ottley, Jr., Atlanta
Virginia H. Ottley, Atlanta
Marie Wikstrom Ovrevik, Brooks
June Owens, Zephry Hills, Florida
Byron Ashley Parker, Sr., Jackson
Arliss E. Paul, Lawrenceville
Evelyn Hoge Pendley, Rome
Patricia Morton Posey, Stone Mountain
Robert E. Price, College Park
Kay Kempton Raade, Brunswick
Zhanna P. Rader, Athens
Rhoda Rainbow, Brooklyn, New York
Jack A. Ransbottom, Ellenwood
Jean Ransbottom, Ellenwood
Eliza Britt Ray, Tifton
Evelyn Sewell Rineer, Cairo
Dorothy P. Ringsrud, Milledgeville
Donald D. Russ, Marietta
William E. Scott, Marietta
Bettie M. Sellers, Young Harris
Harry B. Shaw, Decatur
Jeanne Osborne Shaw, Decatur
Polly K. Shaw, St. Simons Island
Catherine B. Shealy, Atlanta
William A. Simpson, Fort Valley
David T. Smith, Atlanta
Grace Haynes Smith, Plant City, Florida
Maurine S. Smith, Tahlequah, Oklahoma
Thomas C. Smith, Fayetteville
Bruce Souders, Winchester, Virginia
Thomas Paul Spahos, Parris Island, South Carolina
Leland Staven, Rome
Ralph N. Stephens, Athens
Klea V. Stillwell, Marietta
Rebekah Stion, Cairo
Jackie A. Strange, Arlington, Virginia
Eileen H. Stratidakis, Atlanta

Paula L. Sticklin, Marietta
Denver E. Stull, Forest Park
Mark Swanson, Clayton
Letitia Sweitzer, Atlanta
Geri Taran, Marietta
James F. Terrell, Winder
Katharine Theiling, Augusta
Thomas Theus, LaFayette
Ovelle Thomas, Summerville
J. Harold Thurmond, Winder
Ruth L. Tiller, Atlanta
Judy Tisdale, Morrow
Herbert E. Trout, Roswell
Mitzi Hughes Trout, Roswell
Charles R. Tucker, Nashville
Memye Curtis Tucker, Marietta
Tommie Wells Ulrich, Chamblee
Emily Blake Vail, Morrow
Daniel Veach, Atlanta
Virginia Cole Veal, Atlanta
Geraldine G. Wade, Kingston
Lorayne G. Wade, Armuchee
Golda F. Walker, Baton Rouge, Louisiana
Betty Abernathy Wallace, Hampton
James E. Warren, Jr., Atlanta
Connie Smith Watson, Fitzgerald
Lillian K. Webb, Marietta
Gus Wentz, Sandy Springs
Jane Eve Wilheit, Gainesville
John W. Williams, Alto
William Henry Williams, Decatur
Ella H. Wilson, Atlanta
Joy B. Wix, Atlanta
Harriet Fay Woodcock, Gainesville
Dorothy W. Worth, Decatur
Terry Young, Roswell
E. Jerome Zeller, Summerville
Patricia B. Zeller, Summerville

IN RETROSPECT—1989–90 in
GEORGIA STATE POETRY SOCIETY

Georgia State Poetry Society, Inc., launched its second decade of organization with the year beginning July 1, 1989. Continuing proven programs from the first ten years of work, the Society promoted poetic creativity through quarterly contests for members and other poets, sponsored the Youth Poetry Awards for Georgia students, and conducted the Byron Herbert Reece International Awards. The entries judged prize winners in these poetry awards are included in *The Reach of Song, 1989–1990*. This anthology, also a continuing project of the Society since its founding, is in itself an attestation to the objective of stimulating a finer and more intelligent appreciation of poetry.

Quarterly meetings provide opportunities for members and guests to study poetry and give incentives for practice in the writing of poetry. The meetings during 1989–90 had some outstanding poets as speakers.

The summer 1989 meeting was held at the New Perry Hotel, Perry, Georgia, with Judson Mitcham of Macon as speaker. He views poetry as "very private works of the heart. Each is a little death and is far less alive on the page than when written. Each poem is a prayer."

The fall, winter and spring meetings were held at the student center, Mercer University, Atlanta. The October meeting featured Robert Earl Price, Artistic Associate with Atlanta's Seven Stages Theatre. A playwright, filmmaker, and poet, he stated, "Poems have the power to release the strength of the repressed spirit of poor and oppressed people. I write poems intended to change the world."

The winter meeting on January 20, 1990, had a morning workshop led by Anthony Harrington. His emphasis was on "Verse as the Ground of Poetry," giving a strong plea for a return to traditional forms, meter and rhyme in poetry. The afternoon speaker was member Bettie Sellers who read from her own works and related the finished poem with strong personal experiences.

The April speaker was Anthony Grooms, assistant professor of creative writing at the University of Georgia and a young poet of note. He read from his latest book, *Ice Poems*.

The summer 1990 meeting was held at Truett McConnell College, Cleveland, on August 11. Georgia novelist, journalist, documentarist and poet, Philip Lee Williams of Athens, told of his motivation for writing and read from his forthcoming book of poems, *Night Flight*. The quarterly meetings brought a wide variety of talent and expertise from speakers who sought to enlighten, inform and encourage members to more productive poetry writing.

Dr. Frank McKemie ended a two-year term as president of the Society on June 30, 1990. Officers serving with him were Dr. Edward DeZurko, vice-president; Neil Fraser, secretary; and Harry Shaw, treasurer. Dr. McKemie was honored with a plaque commending his faithful service. The officers installed for the 1990–91 year are Ethelene Dyer Jones, president; Dr. Edward DeZurko, vice-president; Nancy Klotz, secretary; and John K. Ottley, Jr., treasurer.

Founding president, Edward Davin Vickers, died on April 17, 1990 after an extended illness. At the April 21 meeting of the Society, tributes in memory of Mr. Vickers were read by Jo Ann Yeager Adkins, Ethelene Dyer Jones and Rebekah Stion. An Edward Davin Vickers Memorial Fund established by the Society will be used to finance an international poetry award to honor the founding president. Noted for his organizational skills and his ability to bring persons together to foster the art of poetry, Mr. Vickers will be remembered as a poet of note and as the guiding influence in the Society's first ten years of operation.

Winner of the first chapbook contest sponsored by Georgia State Poetry Society was member Patricia Canterbury of Sacramento, California. For members only, the chapbook entries were judged by Mary Snotherly of Raleigh, North Carolina. Entitled *Shadowdrifters: Images of China*, Mrs. Canterbury's work was described by the judge as being "richly told poems . . . well-crafted, and on the page, pleasing to the eye. Many of the poems seem to spin off from 'discovery' . . . our like human condition is ever in sight." The Society published 300 copies of the chapbook, 250 of which were awarded to the winner, with fifty retained to be sold by the Society to help defray chapbook publication costs.

The quarterly newsletter poetry contest chaired by Julia Evatt featured the poems of one or two winners each quarter. The poem named "best of the year" was "The Maestro's Hands" by Grace Haynes Smith of Plant City, Florida.

A popular segment of each quarter's meetings is announcement of winners in contests. Marthalou Hunter chaired the general contests for 1989–90. The prize-winning poems are published in this edition of *Reach of Song*.

Herbert Walter Denmark was chairman for members' readings at Society meetings. Both beginning and professional poets shared their poetic ventures in an appreciative environment.

Another means of encouraging member creativity is through review of their published books of poetry. Virginia Veal led the book reviews at quarterly meetings. Members' publications were added to the Georgia State Poetry Society Library located at Mercer University in Atlanta.

The work of the Society in any given year is the combination of many persons contributing ideas in quarterly Board of Directors' meetings and then working to implement plans through programs and services of the Society. A strong feature of the Georgia State Poetry Society is the dedication and commitment of volunteers who labor to bring about the Society's goals.

Affiliation with the National Federation of State Poetry Societies and the Academy of American Poets broadens the scope of interest beyond the state level. Membership provides individuals a camaraderie and group experience in the art and promotion of poetry. The year 1989–90 ended with many goals accomplished and a total membership of 244. Programs of the Society are funded in part by the Georgia Council for the Arts through an appropriation from the Georgia General Assembly and the National Endowment for the Arts.

by Ethelene Dyer Jones

POET INDEX TO PRIZE POEMS